DEVELOPMENT
IN   PRACTICE

Toward
Gender Equality

Toward
Gender Equality

The Role of Public Policy

THE WORLD BANK
WASHINGTON, D.C.

The Development in Practice series publishes reviews of the World
Bank's activities in different regions and sectors. It lays particular
emphasis on the progress that is being made and on the policies and
practices that hold the most promise of success in the effort to reduce
poverty in the developing world.

This book is a product of the staff of the World Bank, and the judgments
made herein do not necessarily reflect the views of its Board of Executive
Directors or the countries they represent.

Photo credits: Maurice Asseo

Library of Congress Cataloging-in-Publication Data

Toward gender equality : the role of public policy.
        p.   cm. — (Development in practice)
    Includes bibliographical references (p. 70).
    ISBN 0-8213-3337-2
    1. Women—Government policy. 2. Women's rights. 3. Sex
discrimination against women. 4. Economic development. I. Series:
Development in practice (Washington, D.C.)
HQ1236.T68   1995
305.4—dc20   95-631
                                                      CIP

Contents

Foreword

TWENTY years ago in Mexico the First World Conference on Women inspired a movement that has helped to reduce gender inequality worldwide. Illiteracy among women is declining, maternal mortality and total fertility rates are beginning to fall, and more women are participating in the labor force than ever before. However, much remains to be done.

In low-income countries women are often denied health care and basic education. Worldwide, women face limited access to financial services, technology, and infrastructure. They are locked into relatively low-productivity work. In addition to performing household tasks and child-rearing duties, women work longer hours for lower pay than most men. And, most discouraging of all, hundreds of thousands of women each year are subject to gender-related violence.

Persistent inequality between women and men constrains a society's productivity and, ultimately, slows its rate of economic growth. Although this problem has been generally recognized, evidence on the need for corrective action is more compelling today than ever.

This report, written for the Fourth World Conference on Women, is intended as a reference to strategies for promoting gender equality and, consequently, enhancing economic efficiency. It pulls together evidence, including case studies, that demonstrates the need for government action to improve the economic status of women. It points out how public policy can and should support services and infrastructure that provide the highest social returns and that are most heavily used by women. The report also aims to stimulate creative solutions to the problem of gender inequality by highlighting innovative and sometimes not obvious strategies that have proved successful. A study in Morocco, for instance, shows that paving public roads to schools increases by 40 percent the probability that local girls will attend classes.

Policy reform that provides an enabling environment for economic growth goes hand in hand with investing in people. The success of one strategy draws on the success of the other. No efforts at gender equality, however, can be successful without the participation of women themselves.

As the international community gathers in Beijing for the Fourth World Conference on Women, the World Bank stands ready to assist client governments in response to the challenges ahead. The Bank believes that by advancing gender equality, governments can greatly enhance the future well-being and prosperity of their people.

Armeane M. Choksi
Vice President
Human Capital Development and Operations Policy
The World Bank

Acknowledgments

THIS REPORT was prepared by a team led by Kei Kawabata and comprising Alison Evans, Zafiris Tzannatos, Tara Vishwanath, and Rekha Menon. The work was carried out under the direction of Minh Chau Nguyen and the overall guidance of K. Y. Amoako. Valuable contributions were made by Joyce Cacho, Lionel Demery, Shahid Khandker, and Kalanidhi Subbarao.

Background papers for the report were prepared by team members and by Anjana Bhushan; Lynn Brown and Lawrence Haddad; Florencia Castro-Leal, with Ignacio Tavares and Ramon Lopez; Roberta Cohen; Monica Fong; Roger Key, with Beverly Mullings; Andrew Mason; and Veena Siddharth.

An external review group and a Bankwide advisory committee provided valuable guidance at all stages of the report's preparation. Kalpana Bardhan, Pranab Bardhan, Nancy Folbre, and T. Paul Schultz were the external reviewers. Harold Alderman, Jean-Jacques Dethier, Louise Fox, Sunita Gandhi, Chris Grootaert, Jeffrey Hammer, Tariq Husain, Elizabeth King, Augusta Molnar, Helena Ribe, and Paula Valad made up the advisory committee. The report was edited by Jo Bischoff, Richard M. Crum, and Fiona Mackintosh; Benjamin Crow provided word-processing and graphics support.

The report also reflects the contributions of the participants in consultations held with nongovernmental organizations on March 13, 1995, in New York. Data supplied by the United Nations and its agencies, particularly the International Labour Organization, the United Nations Educational, Scientific, and Cultural Organization (UNESCO), the United Nations Statistical Office, and the World Health Organization, were invaluable for the preparation of the report.

The production of the report was made possible by the assistance of the Norwegian Ministry of Foreign Affairs, which has given unwavering support to the promotion of gender equality.

Definitions and Data Notes

Definitions

Expected number of years of formal schooling. The total number of years of schooling that a child of a certain age can expect to receive if current enrollment patterns remain unchanged.

Literacy rate. The proportion of the adult population that can read or write. This indicator is not always accurate because it is self-reported and represents past investments in schooling. It is often defined only with respect to selected languages and may not take into account the progress being made in many countries through literacy campaigns.

Life expectancy at birth. The number of years a newborn infant would live if prevailing patterns of mortality at the time of birth were to remain unchanged throughout the child's life.

Maternal mortality ratio. The number of women who die in pregnancy and childbirth per 100,000 live births; a measure of the risk that women face of dying from pregnancy-related causes.

Data Notes

Unless otherwise specified, dollar amounts are current U.S. dollars. A billion is a thousand million.

The data used in this report cover a range of time periods and are from more than 100 countries (both developing and industrial).

Unless otherwise specified, geographic regions are those used by the World Bank in its analytical and operational work and are defined as follows:

Sub-Saharan Africa: all countries south of the Sahara except South Africa.

East Asia and the Pacific: low- and middle-income economies of East and Southeast Asia and the Pacific.

Europe and Central Asia: middle-income European countries and the countries that formed the former Soviet Union.

Latin America and the Caribbean: all American and Caribbean economies south of the United States.

Middle East and North Africa: all the economies of North Africa and the Middle East.

South Asia: Bangladesh, Bhutan, India, Myanmar, Nepal, Pakistan, and Sri Lanka.

Summary

THREE messages echo throughout this document:

- The causes of gender inequality are complex, linked as they are to the intrahousehold decisionmaking process. However the decisions are made, the intrahousehold allocation of resources is influenced by market signals and institutional norms that do not capture the full benefits to society of investing in women. Low levels of education and training, poor health and nutritional status, and limited access to resources depress women's quality of life and hinder economic efficiency and growth.
- It is therefore essential that public policies work to compensate for market failures in the area of gender equality. These policies should equalize opportunities between women and men and redirect resources to those investments with the highest social returns. Of these investments, female education, particularly at the primary and lower-secondary level, is the most important, as it is the catalyst that increases the impact of other investments in health, nutrition, family planning, agriculture, industry, and infrastructure.
- Women themselves are agents for change because they play a key role in shaping the welfare of future generations. Public policies cannot be effective without the participation of the target group—in this case, women, who make up more than half the world's people. Their views need to be incorporated into policy formulation.

Progress to Date

Over the past two decades considerable progress has been made in reducing the gender gap worldwide.

- In 1960, for every 100 boys enrolled in primary school, there were 65 girls. In 1990 the ratio had risen to 85.
- In 1980 an average six-year-old girl in a developing country could expect to attend school for 7.3 years. By 1990 this figure had increased to 8.4 years.
- Since the 1950s the female labor force has grown twice as fast as the male labor force. Worldwide, more than 40 percent of women over 15 years of age are now in the labor force; in developing countries women account for 30 percent of the labor force. (These figures, it should be noted, do not fully reflect women's participation in the informal sector or as unpaid family members in agriculture.)

Nevertheless, inequalities between men and women persist in many important areas.

- Despite women's biological advantage, their mortality and morbidity rates frequently exceed those of men, particularly during childhood and the reproductive years.
- Traditionally, women are employed in lower-paying jobs and in a narrower range of occupations than are men. Women's wages are typically only 60–70 percent of wages earned by men.
- Whether in private sector employment or public sector decisionmaking, women are less likely to be in positions of responsibility than are men.

Why Do Gender Inequalities Persist?

The causes of the persistent inequality between men and women are only partially understood. In recent years attention has focused on inequalities in the allocation of resources at the household level, as seen in the higher share of education, health, and food expenditures boys receive in comparison with girls. The decisionmaking process within households is complex and is influenced by social and cultural norms, market opportunities, and institutional factors. There is considerable proof that the intrahousehold allocation of resources is a key factor in determining the levels of schooling, health, and nutrition accorded household members.

Inequalities in the allocation of household resources matter because education, health, and nutrition are strongly linked to well-being, economic efficiency, and growth. Low levels of educational attainment and poor health and nutrition aggravate poor living conditions and reduce an individual's capacity to work productively. Such economic inefficiency represents a significant loss to society and hampers future economic growth.

Social returns to investments in women's education and health
are significantly greater than for similar investments in men.

The social and economic losses are greatest when women are denied access to basic education and health care. Data from around the world show that private returns to investments in education are the same for women as for men and may even be marginally higher (Psacharopoulos 1994). More importantly, social returns (that is, total benefits to society) to investments in women's education and health are significantly greater than for similar investments in men, largely because of the strong correlation between women's education, health, nutritional status, and fertility levels and the education, health, and productivity of future generations. These correlations are even stronger when women have control over the way resources are allocated within the household.

Wage differentials between women and men in the market are closely linked to educational levels and work experience. Since, on average, women earn 30–40 percent less than men, it is not surprising that fewer women than men participate in the labor force. This wage disparity, reinforced by discriminatory institutional norms, in turn influences the intrahousehold division of resources. A vicious circle ensues as households invest less in daughters than in sons in the belief that investment in girls yields fewer benefits. As a result, many women are unable to work outside the household because they lack the education or experience that men have.

The decision not to participate in the labor force does not necessarily reflect a woman's own choice, nor does it always correspond to the optimum use of household resources. Furthermore, the market wage does not take into account the social benefits of educating and hiring women. Discrimination in households and in the market carries not only private costs for individuals and households but social costs for society as well.

Public policies for reducing gender inequalities are therefore essential for counteracting market failure and improving the well-being of all members of society. Investing in women's education and health expands their choices in labor markets and other income-generating activities and increases the rate of return on a household's most valuable asset—its labor.

The decision to allocate women's time to the type of nonwage work women typically carry out within the household, such as child care, food preparation, and, in low-income countries especially, subsistence farming and the collection of fuelwood and water, has less to do with economics than with social conventions and norms. These norms can have a strong influence on the household division of labor, even in industrial economies, where women's levels of human capital are equal to—and sometimes higher than—those of most men.

The economy pays for this inequality in reduced labor productivity today and diminished national output tomorrow.

Whether this division of labor is appropriate is, essentially, for society to decide. However, there is no doubt that women's entry into the labor market and other spheres of the economy is directly affected by the extensive amounts of time they traditionally devote to household maintenance and family care. Most men do not make similar allocations of time in the home. Such inequality constrains women's employment choices and can limit girls' enrollment in schools. The economy pays for this inequality in reduced labor productivity today and diminished national output tomorrow. Public policy can address inequalities in the household division of labor by supporting initiatives that reduce the amount of time women spend doing unpaid work. Examples of such interventions include improved water and sanitation services, rural electrification, and better transport infrastructure.

Constraints on female employment opportunities arising from the household division of labor are compounded by institutional norms operating within the labor market. Although overt wage discrimination is illegal in many countries, employers frequently segregate jobs or offer less training to women workers. Employers often perceive the returns to investing in women workers as lower than those for men, mainly because of women's primary role in childrearing.

Lack of access to financial services, to land, and to information and technology compounds the unequal treatment of women. Requirements for collateral, high transaction costs, and limited mobility and education contribute to women's inability to obtain credit. When women do have access to credit, the effect on household and individual well-being is striking. Borrowing by women is linked to increased holdings of nonland assets, to improvements in the health status of female children, and to an increased probability that girls will enroll in school. Independent access to land is associated with higher productivity and, in some cases, with greater investments by women in land conservation.

Strategies for the Future

If the benefits from investing in girls and women are so great and can be quantified, why do households and employers underinvest in women? The main reason is that, as discussed above, markets fail to capture the full benefit to society of investing in women and girls. Where the market fails or is absent, government must take the lead. Public policy can contribute, directly and indirectly, to reducing gender inequalities by, for example:

- Modifying the legal and regulatory framework to ensure equal opportunities
- Ensuring macroeconomic stability and improving microeconomic incentives
- Redirecting public policies and public expenditures to those investments with the highest social returns
- Adopting targeted interventions that correct for gender inequalities at the microlevel.

Modifying the law to eliminate gender discrimination and equalize opportunities for women and men is an important first step. However, legal reform by itself does not ensure equal treatment. Further public action is required to make sure that gender-neutral laws are enforced at the national and local levels.

Sound economic policies and well-functioning markets are essential for growth, employment generation, and the creation of an environment in which the returns to investing in women and girls can be fully realized. Economic instability and price distortions can hinder the process. Consequently, sound macroeconomic management is critical. In general, two sets of policies are necessary: one emphasizing macroeconomic stability and the elimination of price distortions, the other focusing on labor-demanding growth and a reorientation in public spending toward basic services with high social returns—such as education, health care, and water supply.

Gender inequalities in the distribution of the benefits of public spending frequently arise because of a bias within households that limits women's access to publicly provided services. In addition, the services provided by public spending often are of less benefit to women than to men. Public policy can help remedy this problem by rearranging expenditure priorities among sectors and within the social sectors. It can ensure support for those services and types of infrastructure that offer the highest social returns to public spending and that are most heavily used by women and children, such as water supply and sanitation services and rural electrification.

Finally, general policy interventions may not be enough, and programs that specifically target women and girls may be required. Targeting is justi-

Governments can no longer afford not to invest in women.

fiable on two grounds. First, because women are disproportionately represented among the poor, targeting women can be an effective strategy for
reducing poverty (broadly defined to include limited access to services, resources, and other capability-enhancing factors). Second, where gender differences are wide, targeting—for example, the provision of stipends so that
girls can attend school—may be needed to capture social gains and increase
internal efficiency.

Conclusion

Governments can no longer afford not to invest in women. The evidence on
the high private and social returns to investments in women and girls cannot
be ignored. By directing public resources toward policies and projects that
reduce gender inequality, policymakers not only promote equality but also
lay the groundwork for slower population growth, greater labor productivity,
a higher rate of human capital formation, and stronger economic growth.
However, none of these developments can be sustained without the participation of women themselves. Governments and collaborating institutions must
listen more carefully to the voices of individual women, including
policymakers, and to women's groups. By working with others to identify
and implement policies that promote gender equality, governments can make
a real difference to the future well-being and prosperity of their people.

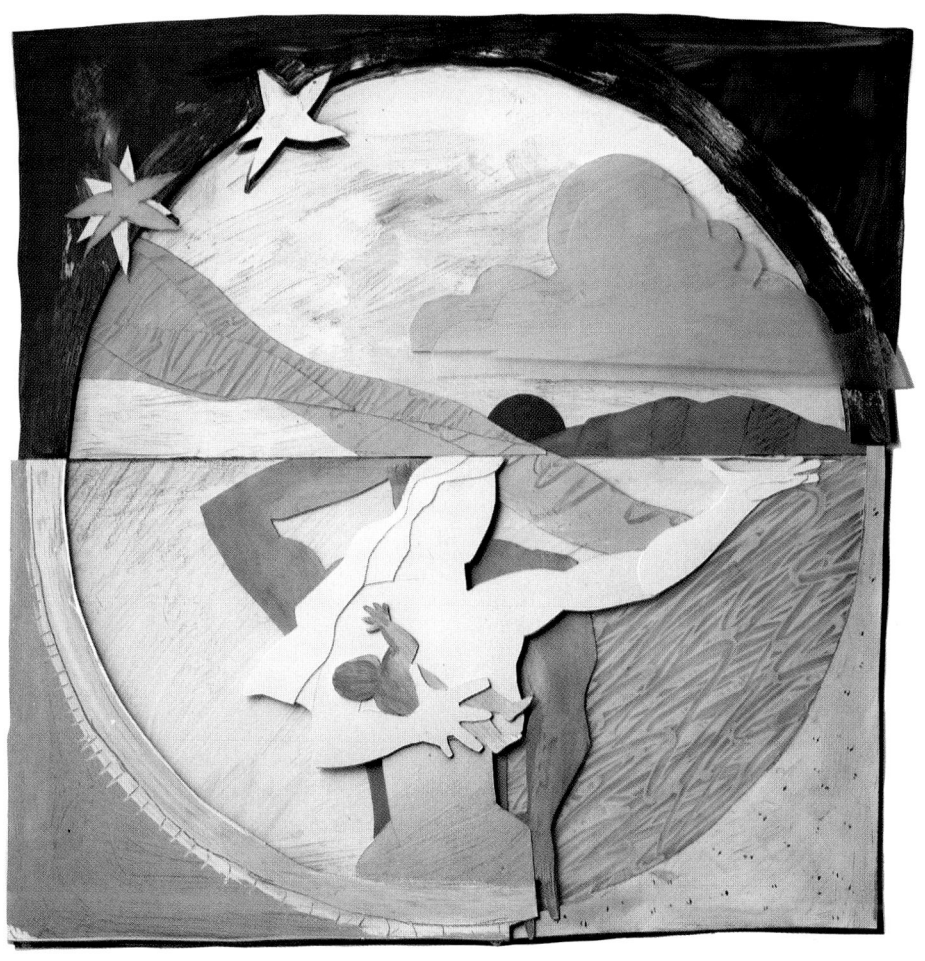

I am the woman who holds up the sky
The rainbow runs through my eyes
The sun makes a path to my womb
My thoughts are in the shape of clouds
But my words are yet to come.

Poem of the Ute Indians

CHAPTER ONE

Gender Inequalities Persist

Although the gap between opportunities for men and women is narrowing, inequalities persist, especially in certain regions. This report examines four major development indicators: educational attainment, maternal mortality, life expectancy, and economic participation outside the household. All four are closely related to each other and in turn are closely correlated with individual well-being. These indicators provide a broad picture of trends in gender inequality and their impact on the relative well-being of women and of men.

Education

Despite the progress in raising educational enrollment rates for both males and females across all regions in the past three decades, growth in educational opportunities at all levels for females lags behind that for males (figure 1.1). In 1990 an average six-year-old girl in a developing country could expect to attend school for 8.4 years. The figure had increased from 7.3 years in 1980—but an average boy of the same age in a developing country could expect to attend school for 9.7 years. The gender gap in expected years of schooling is widest in some countries in South Asia, the Middle East, and Sub-Saharan Africa (see figure 1.2). Gender differences in access to education are usually worse in minority populations such as refugees and internally displaced persons, of which only a few children go to school.

The Gender Gap in Education Has Narrowed.

FIGURE 1.1   SCHOOL ENROLLMENT RATIOS IN DEVELOPING COUNTRIES

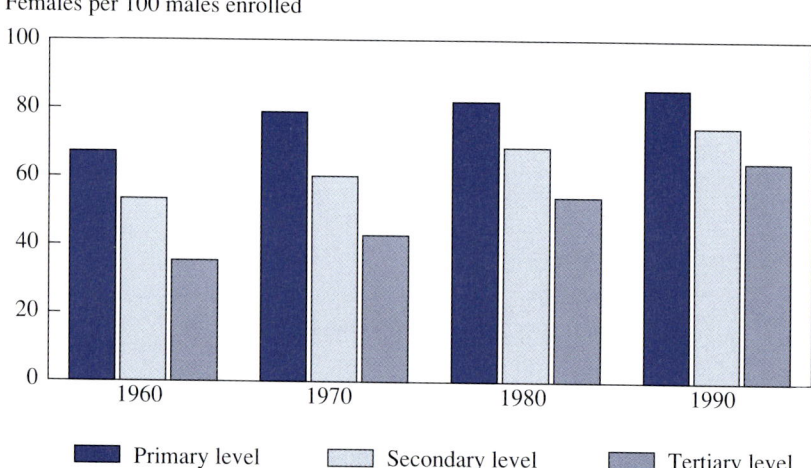

Females per 100 males enrolled

Sources: UNESCO, *Statistical Yearbook, 1991;* World Bank staff estimates.

The latest available figures show that 77 million girls of primary school age (6–11 years) are not in school, compared with 52 million boys (figure 1.3). Moreover, even these gross enrollment rates often mask high absenteeism and high dropout rates. Dropout rates are notably high in low-income countries but vary by gender worldwide and within regions. The rates for girls tend to be linked to age, peaking at about grade 5 and remaining high at the secondary level (Herz and others 1991). Cultural factors, early marriage, pregnancy, and household responsibilities affect the likelihood that girls will remain in school.

Although the gross enrollment rate is an acceptable indicator of progress in education, most studies use literacy rates as an indicator of well-being. Overall illiteracy rates have decreased among adults in low- and middle-income countries, but the percentage of illiterate women in the world is still higher than the percentage of illiterate men. Older women constitute the largest share of the illiterates in the world today, a consequence of past inequalities in access to education. In Sub-Saharan Africa, the Middle East, and South Asia more than 70 percent of women age 25 and older are illiterate (United Nations 1991).

At postsecondary levels, where the gap in enrollment between women and men is wider, there is implicit "gender streaming," or sex segregation, by field of study, even in areas with more female than male enrollees. Gender

Boys Spend More Years in School Than Girls.

FIGURE 1.2   EXPECTED YEARS OF SCHOOLING

Male-female gap in expected years of schooling

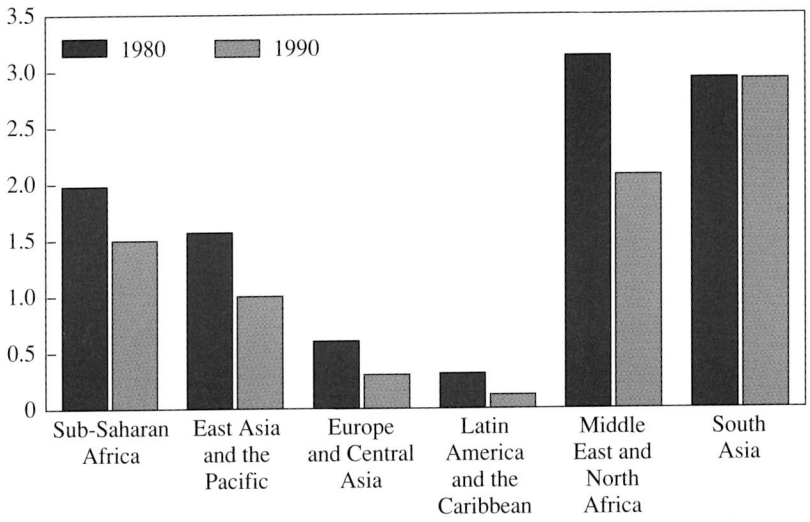

Sources: Donors to African Education 1994; UNESCO 1993a.

streaming, which is widespread in both developing and industrial countries, prevents women from acquiring training in agriculture, forestry, fishing, "hard" sciences, and engineering (figure 1.4).

Health

Over the past two decades life expectancy at birth has increased for both men and women in all regions of the world. In industrial countries women tend to outlive men by six to eight years on average; in low-income countries gender differences are much narrower (two to three years). Despite women's biological advantage, female mortality and morbidity rates frequently exceed those of men, particularly during early childhood and the reproductive years.

During the reproductive period the most important causes of morbidity and mortality among women are high fertility and abortion rates, vulnerability to sexually transmitted diseases (STDs), genital mutilation, and gender violence. Each year, about 500,000 women worldwide die from the complications of pregnancy and childbirth. Maternal mortality ratios for developing

More Girls Than Boys Fail to Attend Primary School.

FIGURE 1.3   CHILDREN NOT IN SCHOOL, 1990

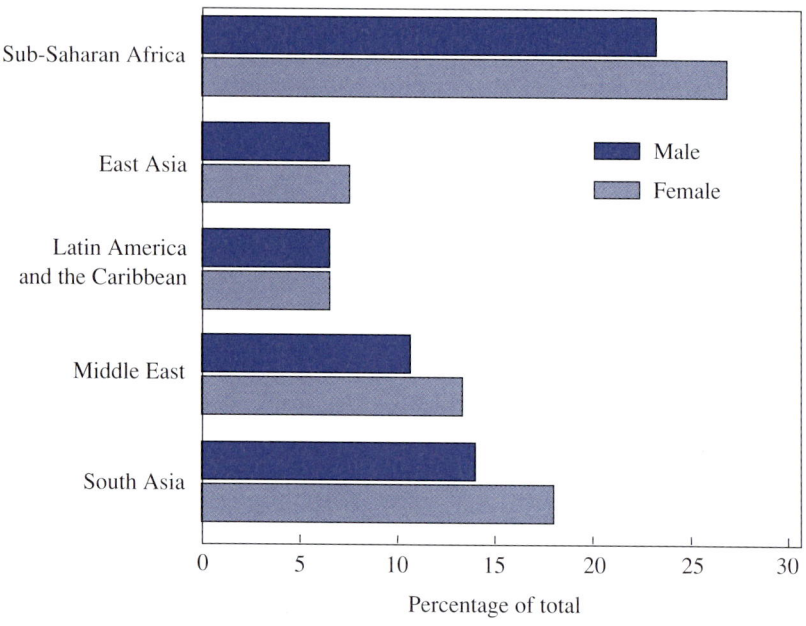

Percentage of total

Source: UNESCO 1993b.

and industrial countries vary greatly; the rates in parts of South Asia are among the world's highest, in some cases exceeding 1,500 per 100,000 live births. In Sub-Saharan Africa, where the ratio is 700 maternal deaths per 100,000 live births, a woman runs a 1-in-22 lifetime risk of dying from pregnancy-related causes, but in northern Europe the risk falls to 10 in 100,000 (United Nations 1993). In the transition economies of Eastern Europe and the former Soviet Union, the rates are around 40 to 50 per 100,000 live births.

A major cause of maternal deaths is complications from unsafe abortions. Abortion-related deaths are highest in South and Southeast Asia, followed by Sub-Saharan Africa and Latin America and the Caribbean. Lack of access to contraceptives can mean that abortion is used as a form of birth control. For example, in parts of Eastern Europe and Central Asia abortions are more numerous than live births (World Bank 1994b), and abortion rates were as high as 1.76 per live birth in Russia prior to the transition.

As increasing numbers of women become aware of and learn to use contraceptives, total fertility rates are falling worldwide. The exception is Sub-Saharan Africa, where the total fertility rate averaged 6.4 between 1985

At the Tertiary Level, Fewer Women Than Men Study Agriculture, Science, and Engineering.

FIGURE 1.4   FIELDS OF STUDY

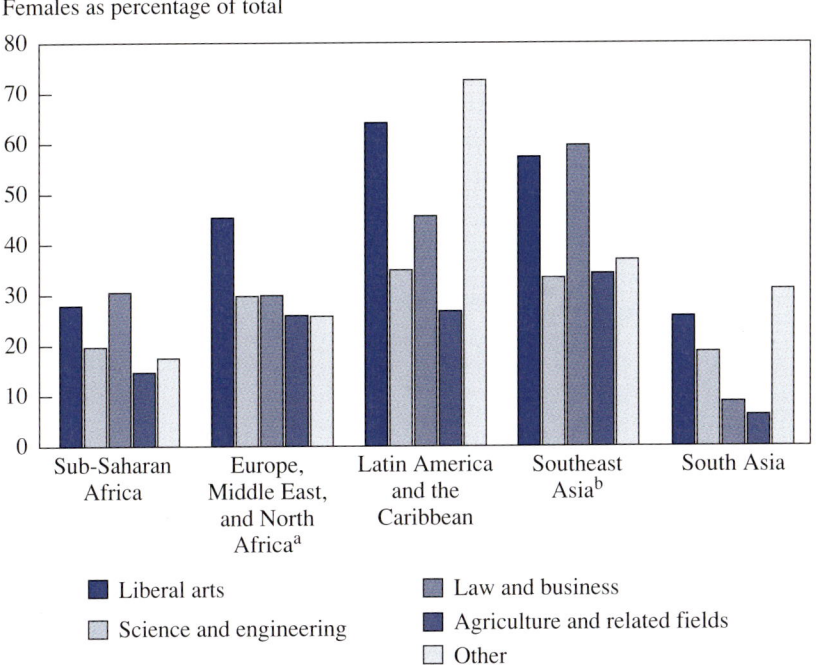

Females as percentage of total

a. Middle-income countries of Europe and all economies of the Middle East and North Africa.
b. Low- and middle-income countries of Southeast Asia.
Source: United Nations, WISTAT database; World Bank staff estimates.

and 1990 and is expected to remain above 6.0 until 2000. High fertility rates and limited use of contraception among women often go hand in hand with high rates of adolescent pregnancies. Every year 15 million teenage women give birth, accounting for one-fifth of all births worldwide (Population Reference Bureau 1994).

Young women are biologically vulnerable to human immunodeficiency virus (HIV) infections and to STDs. Adolescents (age 15–19) and young adults (age 20–24) account for a disproportionate share of the increase in STDs. The incidence of HIV and of acquired immune deficiency syndrome (AIDS) is also increasing among women; already, more than 6 million women worldwide

HIV-Infected Women Are Prevalent in All Regions of the World.

FIGURE 1.5   HIV-INFECTED WOMEN, 1995

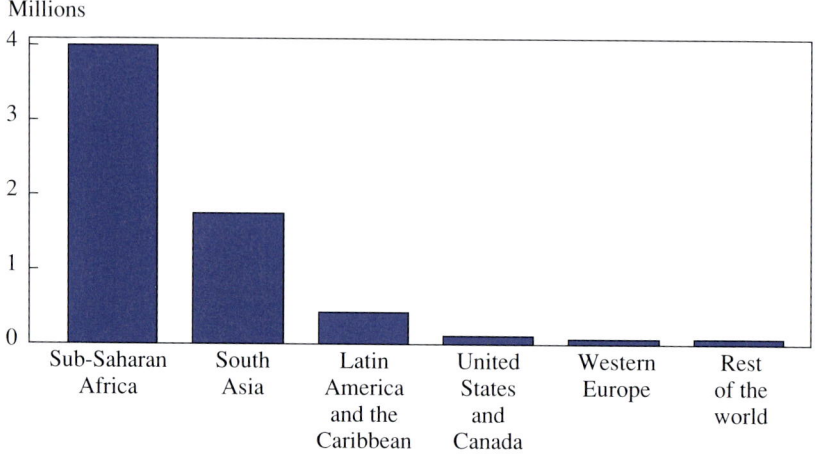

Note: AIDS cases are excluded.
Source: WHO 1994.

have been infected by HIV. The World Health Organization (WHO 1994) estimates that more than 13 million women will have been infected by HIV by
2000 and that about 4 million of that number will have died (figure 1.5). In
Africa, where 10 million adults are infected with the virus, one-half of all
newly infected adults are women, and more than 5 million are women of
childbearing age. In Asia almost half of all adults newly infected with the
virus are women, compared with less than 25 percent just six years ago.

The mortality risk for females is high during the reproductive years, but it
is even higher during infancy and early childhood. Between 1962 and 1992
infant mortality in the developing world decreased by 50 percent (UNICEF
1993). However, in seventeen of the twenty-nine developing countries for
which recent survey data are available, female children age 1–4 were found
to have higher mortality rates than male children, despite girls' biological
advantage (World Bank 1994b). In many of these countries the underlying
cause of high mortality among girls is the parents' bias toward boys, who
receive the best food and medical care.

Genital mutilation, prevalent in twenty-eight countries, is performed on 2
million young girls yearly. The practice leads to long-term morbidity, complications during childbirth, mental trauma, and even death. Table 1.1

summarizes the best available statistics on this practice for selected countries.

Employment and Work

The time women spend on paid and unpaid work is typically greater than the time men spend in the labor market (see table 1.2 for an example). Unpaid family work is rarely recorded in official statistics. It manifests itself only indirectly in the labor market in the form of gender differences in labor force participation rates, sector of employment, hours of work, and wage level.

On the whole, labor force participation rates for women are lower than those for men (figure 1.6). However, these differences are often exaggerated because the definition of the participation rate fails to capture many aspects of women's work, particularly time spent on childbearing, childrearing, and other household tasks. Men are usually in the labor force throughout the prime working years (age 20–60), and their participation rates are typically more than 90 percent in virtually every country. Female participation rates vary widely across countries. In 1990, for every ten men in the labor force there were two women in the Middle East and North Africa, three in South Asia, six in Sub-Saharan Africa, and seven in Southeast Asia (United Nations 1991). Worldwide, 41 percent of women age 15 years or over are in the labor force, but in developing countries the corresponding figure is 31 percent.

These numbers are deceptive, however, because they do not take into account the agricultural work for which women in developing countries are responsible within the family. For example, the Dominican census of 1981 reported that only 21 percent of rural women participated in the labor force,

Tens of Millions of Women Suffer Female Genital Mutilation.

TABLE 1.1   FEMALE GENITAL MUTILATION

Country	Estimated prevalence (percent)	Estimated number of women affected (millions)
Djibouti	98	0.2
Egypt	50	13.5
Eritrea	90	1.5
Ethiopia	90	22.5
Kenya	50	6.3
Nigeria	50	29.2
Sierra Leone	90	2.0
Sudan	89	11.8

Source: Toubia 1993, based on Hosken 1992 and other sources.

In Sri Lanka's Dry Zone, Women Work Longer Hours than Men.

TABLE 1.2   DISTRIBUTION OF MONTHLY WORK HOURS
(hours per month)

Activity	Peak season		Slack season	
	Male	Female	Male	Female
Agricultural production	298	299	245	235
Household tasks	90	199	60	220
Fetching water and firewood	30	50	30	60
Social and religious duties	8	12	15	15
Total work hours	426	560	350	530
Leisure and sleep	294	160	370	190

Source: Wickramasinghe 1992.

but just three years later a special study suggested a figure of 84 percent. The census had omitted such activities as cultivating gardens and caring for domestic animals. In India different definitions of what constitutes "work" have resulted in estimated participation rates as low as 13 percent and as high as 88 percent (Beneria 1992).

Women are usually employed in different sectors than men. Most of women's nonagricultural employment is in the service sector, but in developing countries female employment in manufacturing has been increasing and is catching up with female employment in services (ILO/ INSTRAW 1985). Women in manufacturing tend to be concentrated in only a few subsectors; more than two-thirds of the global labor force in garment production is female, and this subsector absorbs almost one-fifth of the female labor force in manufacturing (UNIDO 1993). Men's employment is more evenly distributed across other sectors, such as mining, manufacturing, construction, utilities, and transport.

Over their lifetime, women change their employment status more often than do men. They are also more likely to be self-employed or employed in occupations with flexible hours, such as subcontracted home work. Regardless of the sector in which they are employed, women tend to work in a narrow range of occupations. Only a few women are in high-paying jobs or in positions with significant responsibility. Nearly two-thirds of the women in manufacturing are laborers, machine operators, and production workers; only 5 percent are professional and technical workers and only 2 percent are administrators and managers (UNIDO 1993). However, there are regional differences; women occupy nearly 60 percent of clerical, sales, and service jobs in Latin America and the Caribbean but fewer than 20 percent of similar positions in South Asia, North Africa, and the Middle East (figure 1.7).

Women Everywhere Are Less Likely Than Men To Be in the Labor Force.

FIGURE 1.6   RATES OF PARTICIPATION IN THE LABOR FORCE BY GENDER

Percent

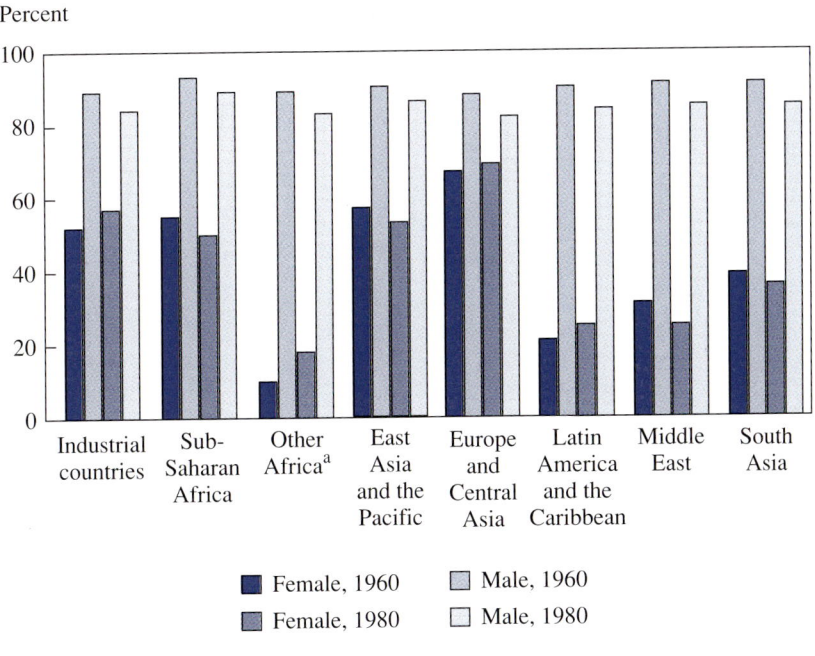

a. Algeria, Egypt, Libya, Morocco, South Africa, and Tunisia.
Source: Sivard 1985.

Wages paid to women are typically about 60–70 percent of those paid to men. About one-quarter of the gender wage gap is explained by differences in educational levels, labor market experience, and other "human capital" characteristics (Psacharopoulos and Tzannatos 1992; Horton 1994). The gender wage gap can also be explained in part by women's lower participation in the labor market—a consequence of domestic and other demands on their time and, possibly, of discriminatory employment practices.

Significant changes in the global economy have affected patterns of employment and working conditions for men and women worldwide. "Globalization" is associated with the deregulation of product and labor markets, with regionalization, and with the liberalization of international trade. In turn, these processes are associated with increased female participa-

Women Tend To Be in Clerical, Sales, and Service Jobs.

FIGURE 1.7   TYPES OF JOBS HELD BY WOMEN

Percentage of total employment in the group

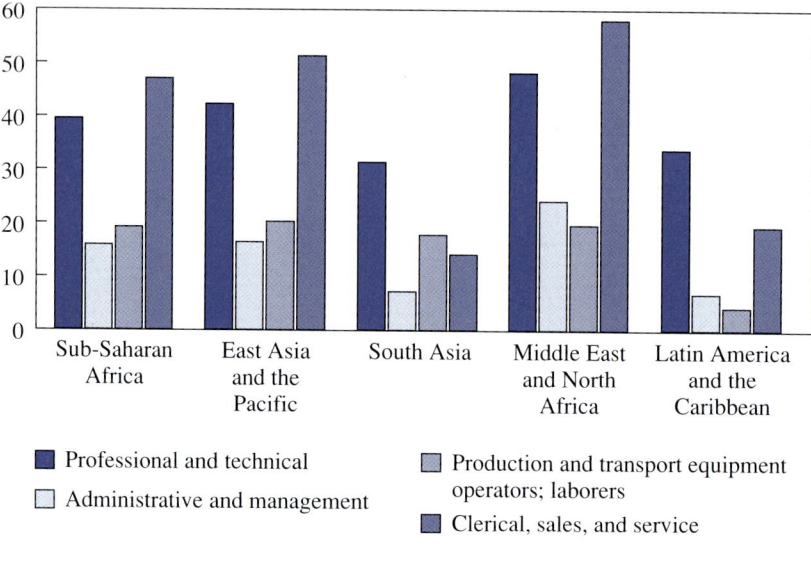

■ Professional and technical   □ Production and transport equipment
□ Administrative and management   operators; laborers
                                       ■ Clerical, sales, and service

Source: United Nations, WISTAT database.

tion in the labor force and with the growing "casualization" of employment, as seen in the growth of part-time work in industrial economies. However, the net effect of globalization on women workers is not yet clear. Growth in the international traded service sector (for example, banking and telecommunications) seems to have offered women in developing countries greater employment opportunities. In addition, the participation rate of women in manufacturing jobs has increased faster than that of men. Women's average participation in the manufacturing labor force is now around 30 percent for both developing and industrial countries.

Worldwide, the number of women employed in export manufacturing has been increasing rapidly, even though this sector employs only a small fraction of all women workers. In Mexico, for example, the number of women employed in export manufacturing rose by nearly 15 percent a year in the 1980s (Jurisman and Moreno 1990). However, employment in this sector has been increasing more rapidly for men than for women, partly because of technological upgrading over time and partly because women are less educated and tend to remain in low-skill occupations (Baden 1993).

Women now account for a growing share of wage employment, and they tend to stay longer in the labor force than ever before.

Despite persistent gender inequalities in the labor market, some recent trends are encouraging. Increasing educational opportunities and decreasing fertility rates have led to an increase in the number of women entering the labor market. Since the 1950s the female labor force has expanded twice as fast as the male labor force. Women now account for a growing share of wage employment, and they tend to stay longer in the labor force than ever before. The narrowing of the gender gap in labor force participation is enabling women to accumulate the work experience necessary for improving their job opportunities and increasing their earnings. In the formal sector more and more women are working in occupations and sectors once dominated by men, and in many countries women's wages relative to men's have increased over time.

The data in this chapter illustrate some aggregate trends, but they cannot tell us anything about the processes behind the persistence of gender inequality. For a more detailed look at these processes, we turn in the next chapter to a growing body of empirical evidence generated at the household and enterprise level. These studies provide a telling insight into the way in which gender inequalities are being challenged, particularly by women themselves. At the same time, these inequalities are reinforced by economic, legal, and cultural incentive systems that discriminate against women. Discrimination continues despite compelling evidence showing that less inequality, especially within the household, is associated with better welfare outcomes for children and better economic outcomes for the household as a whole.

CHAPTER TWO

Gender Inequalities Hamper Growth

INEQUALITY between women and men limits productivity and ultimately slows economic growth. Early empirical studies (for example, Kuznets 1955) suggested that income inequality would increase with economic growth during the initial phases of development. This chapter, however, starts with the hypothesis that there is not necessarily a tradeoff between inequality and growth and, indeed, that high inequality, especially as it affects human capital, hampers growth (Fields 1992; Birdsall and Sabot 1994).[1]

Both theory and empirical evidence point to the importance of human capital in creating the necessary conditions for productivity growth and in reducing aggregate inequality in the future. In addition, women's human capital generates benefits for society in the form of lower child mortality, higher educational attainment, improved nutrition, and reduced population growth. Inequalities in the accumulation and use of human capital are related to lower economic and social well-being for all.

Household and Intrahousehold Resource Allocation

In recent years, attempts to explain persistent gender inequalities in the accumulation and use of human capital have focused on the key role of household decisionmaking and the process of resource allocation within households. Households do not make decisions in isolation, however; their decisions are linked to market prices and incentives and are influenced by cultural, legal, and state institutions. These institutions indirectly affect not only the returns on household investments but also access to productive resources and employment outside the household.

Household decisions about the allocation of resources have a profound effect on the schooling, health care, and nutrition children receive. The mechanisms used to make these decisions and the effect of the decisions on the well-being of individual household members are not fully understood. Two frameworks for thinking about household decisions are the unitary household model and the collective household model (see box 2.1).

BOX 2.1 TWO MODELS OF HOUSEHOLD DECISIONMAKING

The *unitary household model* assumes that household members pool resources and allocate them according to a common set of objectives and goals. Households maximize the joint welfare of their members by allocating income and other resources to the individuals and enterprises that promise the highest rate of return, as reflected in prices and wages. An increase in household income increases the well-being of all household members.

Policy interventions based on the unitary household model aim to increase household welfare, but they do not necessarily affect all household members in the same way. Some household members may be worse off, for example, if they lose control over certain resources; others may be better off, in which case household welfare is not maximized.

Under the *collective household model,* the welfare of individual household members is not synonymous with overall household welfare. Resources are not necessarily pooled, and the household acts as a collective, with members having their own preferences. Decisions on allocating resources reflect market rates of return, but they also mirror the relative bargaining power of household members within the collective (Manser and Brown 1980; McElroy and Horney 1981). Bargaining power is a function of social and cultural norms, as well as of such external factors as opportunities for paid work, laws governing inheritance, and control over productive assets and property rights. These factors influence the terms governing household members' access to resources and decisions about how those resources are used within the household. Thus, an increase in household income may benefit some household members but leave others unaffected or worse off. The outcome depends on a member's ability to exercise control over resources both inside and outside the household, and it cannot be assumed that individual well-being increases as household income rises. (Collective household models do not exclude the possibility that the unitary model may be the best approximation of household decisionmaking in some contexts.)

The collective household model helps explain why gender inequalities persist even though household incomes increase over time. The next sections adopt a collective household framework to explain how these inequalities exact costs in forgone productivity, reduced welfare for individuals and households, and, ultimately, slower economic growth.

Gender Inequalities in Human Capital

There are strong complementarities between education, health, and nutrition, on the one hand, and increased well-being, labor productivity, and growth, on the other. Inequalities in resource allocation that limit household members' educational opportunities, access to health care, or nutrition are costly to individuals, households, and the economy as a whole.

Linkages between Education, Health, and Nutrition

At the household level, gender differences in access to education are closely related to inequalities in the shares of household education expenditures allocated to boys and to girls. This finding stands even though private returns to girls' schooling are similar to, or marginally higher than, those to boys' schooling (figure 2.1; see also Schultz 1988; Mwabu 1994). In this case,

Private Returns to Girls' Education Are High.

FIGURE 2.1   PRIVATE RETURNS TO EDUCATION

Rate of return (percent)

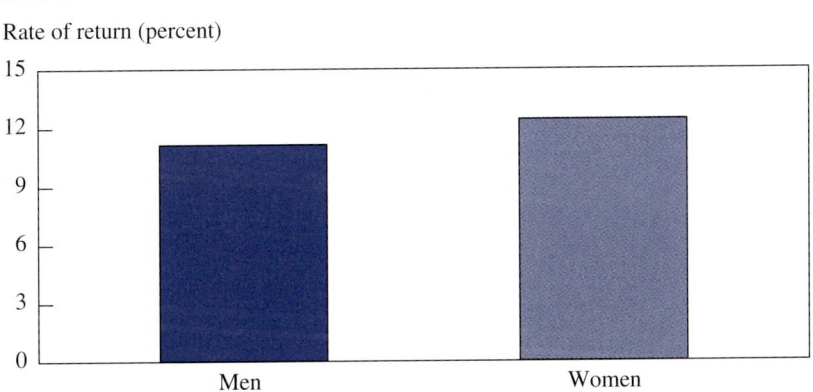

Note: Mincerian method.
Source: Psacharopoulos 1994.

Educated Women Have Fewer, but Healthier, Children.

FIGURE 2.2   EDUCATION, FERTILITY, AND CHILD MORTALITY

Total fertility rate

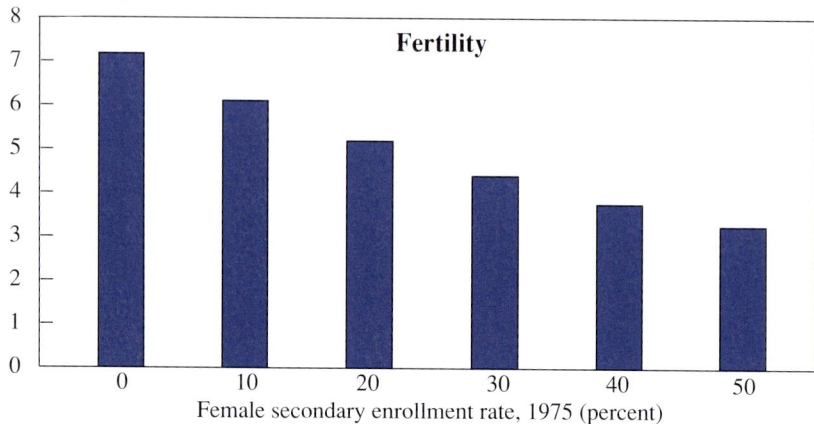

Under 5 mortality per 1,000 live births

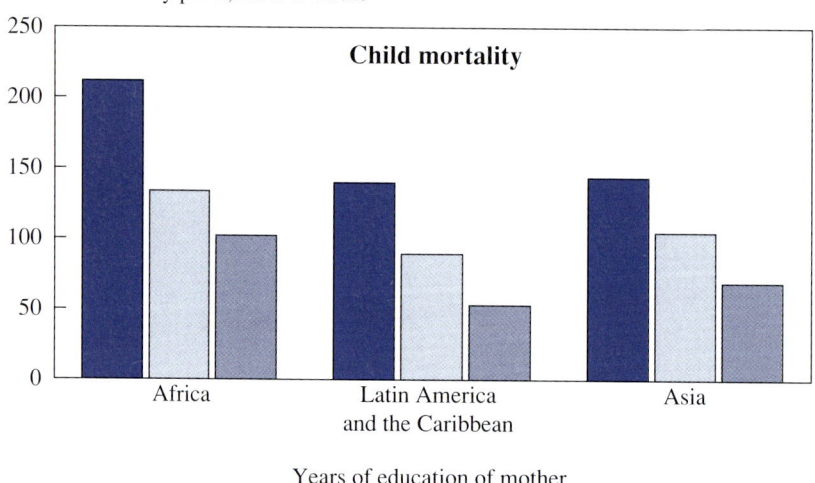

Note: Averages of household survey results.
Sources: For fertility, Subbarao and Raney 1993; for child mortality, Summers 1994.

parental choice reflects the relatively greater restrictions on educational opportunities and employment choices for girls, in comparison with boys, and cultural norms on the appropriate role for girls within the household.

More importantly, the social externalities linked to female education are crucial. Evidence from a large number of countries shows that female education is linked with better health for women and their children and with lower fertility levels (figure 2.2). This link stems from the direct effect of education on the value of a woman's time and, consequently, on private returns to her labor. It also stems from the indirect effect of education on the average age at which women marry, on their knowledge of basic health care and nutrition, and on reproductive choices (Rosenzweig and Schultz 1982, 1987).

Educating girls and women reduces maternal mortality and fertility rates and increases the demand for health services. A simulation study of seventy-two developing countries shows that, with all other factors held constant, a doubling of female secondary school enrollments in 1975 would have reduced the average fertility rate in 1985 from 5.3 to 3.9 children per household and would have lowered the number of births by 29 percent (Subbarao and Raney 1993). Studies for individual countries have found that one additional year of female schooling can reduce the fertility rate, on average, between 5 and 10 percent (Summers 1994).

Women are more vulnerable than men to micronutrient deficiencies that aggravate poor health (World Bank 1994b). Poor health and nutrition reduce productivity and the chances of reaping gains from investment in education. Intrahousehold inequalities in consumption and nutritional allocations can therefore be a signal of inefficiency. Recent estimates suggest that the combined effects on morbidity and mortality of just three types of deficiency—in vitamin A, iodine, and iron—could waste as much as 5 percent of gross domestic product (GDP), yet correcting these deficiencies would cost less than 0.3 percent of low-income countries' GDP (World Bank 1994c, pp. 50–51). Studies of women tea producers in Sri Lanka and of women workers in Chinese cotton mills document the reduction in productivity associated with iron deficiencies and the positive effects of iron supplementation on work and output (Edgerton and others 1979). A study of six villages in Andhra Pradesh, India, found that disabling conditions caused by malnutrition and the prevalence of diseases reduced female labor force participation by 22 percent (Chatterjee 1991).

Physical and mental abuse can also have deleterious effects on the well-being and productivity of women (table 2.1). Violence against women is widespread in all cultures and cuts across all age and income groups. Its consequences include unwanted pregnancy, infection with STDs, miscarriage, partial or permanent disability, and psychological problems such as depression and low self-esteem. Recent World Bank estimates indicate that in both

Violence against Women Starts in the Womb and Continues throughout Life.

TABLE 2.1   VIOLENCE AGAINST WOMEN THROUGH THE LIFE CYCLE

Phase	*Type of violence*
Prebirth	Battering during pregnancy (emotional and physical effects on the women; effects on birth outcomes)
Infancy	Female infanticide; emotional and physical abuse
Girlhood	Sexual abuse by family members and strangers; forced child prostitution
Adolescence	Dating and courtship violence; economically coerced sex; sexual abuse in the workplace; rape; forced prostitution and trafficking in women
Reproductive	Coerced pregnancy; rape; abuse of women by male partners; dowry abuse and murder; partner homicide; psychological abuse; sexual abuse of unmarried and childless women; abuse of women with disabilities

Source: Heise 1993.

industrial and developing countries domestic violence and rape cause women of reproductive age to lose a significant percentage of healthy days. Domestic violence appears to be an example of how the relatively weaker bargaining power of women and the paucity of options for them outside the home can affect the intrahousehold distribution of welfare.

Prospects for gainful employment, as well as the availability of basic social services such as water supply and sanitation, also influence women's well-being. The survival chances of female children in India appear to increase as the employment rate for women rises and the earnings differential between men and women decreases (Bardhan 1988). Dowry and marriage practices, along with household ownership of land, are closely linked to women's chances of survival. The effect of such practices cannot be overestimated. Sen's (1990) comparison of female-male mortality rates in China, India, and Sub-Saharan Africa suggest that more than 100 million women are "missing."

Public spending on social services affects the ability of individuals and households to benefit from their own private spending on human capital. In most industrial countries mortality rates decreased even before modern medical care became widely available, mainly because of improved water supplies and sanitation. The same is likely to hold for the developing world. Public interventions that address market failures—underprovision of water and sanitation facilities and shortages of health services such as immunization and family planning—have a significant effect, and one that is probably greater for women than for men.[2]

Lack of data makes it difficult to evaluate the effects of public spending on the educational attainment and health of women and men. Very little empirical evidence in this area exists, but there is some indication that the proportion of public subsidies for education that benefits females is lower than the proportion that benefits males. In Kenya in 1992–93, for example, public spending on education amounted to the equivalent of an annual subsidy of 605 Kenyan shillings per capita: males received, on average, 670 shillings and females only 543 shillings. In Mexico the gender difference in public education subsidies was somewhat less; in Pakistan males received almost twice the female subsidy. Gender inequalities in the distribution of subsidies are greater at higher than at primary levels. In Pakistan girls receive, on average, only 26 rupees a year for secondary schooling, compared with 58 rupees for boys. Box 2.2 explains how these figures are calculated.

Supply-side differences are partly a function of poorly targeted resources (as, for example, when more is spent on tertiary than on primary schooling). More importantly, they reflect differences in household demand for education for girls and boys. If more girls attended and stayed in school, the proportion of public subsidy going to girls would be greater.

In health care, assessing the incidence of public spending by gender is particularly difficult because of the marked differences in the health needs of women and men. These differences are related to different biological re-

---

BOX 2.2 WHO BENEFITS FROM PUBLIC SPENDING?

Benefit incidence analysis is one method of computing the distribution of public expenditures across different demographic groups. The procedure involves allocating per unit public subsidies (for example, per student for the education sector) according to individual utilization rates of public services (van de Walle and Nead 1995).

Incidence analysis brings together two basic types of information. First, government expenditures for each type of public service are used to compute per unit subsidies. Second, household surveys provide information on utilization rates (school enrollment rates, for example) by gender, expenditure group, and region. Equality in the distribution of expenditures is then analyzed on the basis of the pattern of in-kind subsidies various groups receive. This pattern is defined by two variables: the way services are used and recurrent expenditures.

The main advantage of this type of analysis is that it measures how well public services are targeted to certain groups in the population, including women, the poor, and residents of regions of interest.

quirements and to women's reproductive and childrearing roles. Some evidence suggests that because of these differences, per capita health care subsidies to women are the same as and sometimes larger than those to men. What is clearer is that women are less likely than men to seek health care, including, in many countries, hospital care, when it is needed and are more likely to consult a nonmedical health care worker (rather than a qualified medical practitioner). Education tends to increase the likelihood that women will seek health care, whether public or private (World Bank 1994b).

Increases in women's well-being yield important intergenerational benefits and productivity gains in the future.

The importance of private and public investments in education and health services that will improve women's well-being is clear. These services are also important for another reason: there is considerable evidence that increases in women's well-being yield important intergenerational benefits and productivity gains in the future. World Bank Living Standards Measurement Study (LSMS) surveys carried out in Nicaragua (1993), Viet Nam (1993), Pakistan (1991), and Côte d'Ivoire (1988) suggest that the probability of children being enrolled in school increases with their mother's educational level and that (controlling for income and household size) girls, particularly those in nonpoor households, are more likely to attend school if their mothers attended school.[3] Other studies show that households with educated mothers tend to provide children with greater quantities of more nutritious food, often at a lower cost, than households with poorly educated mothers (Thomas 1990b).

Data from Brazil show that giving women more control over nonlabor income has a larger impact on child anthropometric measures, nutritional intakes, and the proportion of the household budget devoted to human capital inputs than if men had control of this income (Thomas 1991, 1993). Other studies indicate that women spend proportionately more of the income they control on health care for children than do men. Women also spend more on food products (as opposed to such goods as alcohol and tobacco) than men do (Duraiswamy 1992; Hoddinott and Haddad 1992). But fathers' education is also important, especially in interaction with mothers' education (Thomas 1990a). Other studies have shown that children's educational attainment is lowest in households where the male head has no schooling. In Ghana the impact of a mother's education on her children's schooling is reduced when their father has no schooling, even after controlling for income and household size (Lavy 1992).

Maternal health (which is linked to education) also has important intergenerational effects. Children of mothers who are malnourished or sickly or receive inadequate prenatal and delivery care face a greater risk of disease and premature death. Iodine-deficient mothers run a greater risk of giving birth to infants with severe mental retardation and other congenital abnormalities than do healthy mothers. Reduced fertility and improved health for women can increase individual productivity and improve family well-being. When good health is combined with education and access to jobs, the result is higher rates of economic growth.

Household and Labor Market Linkages

The link between the household and the labor market is particularly important. Specialization of labor within the household—whether individually chosen, socially determined, or legally induced—can accentuate gender inequalities in the formal and informal labor markets by leaving most of the unpaid work to women. This situation arises from convention rather than from comparative advantage. Inadequate public and community services, transport, and housing also often have an uneven effect on the way men and women spend their time and can increase the demand for goods produced at home using unpaid labor (Moser 1994). Thus, women may spend as much (or more) time on unpaid work as on market work. In some countries this unpaid work contributes as much as one-third to the economy's recorded GDP—and even more to the welfare of poor families.

The amount of time women contribute to household production and maintenance, direct income generation, and family care combined is widely held to exceed that of men. Analysis of data from Bangladesh, Botswana, Ghana, Kenya, Pakistan, the Philippines, and Zambia on how rural women spend their time confirms that, although use of time by women, and by different generations of women, varies according to location, available technology, household characteristics, and cultural norms, gender bias in time use is widespread.

Women are generally responsible for collecting fuelwood and carrying water. Girls and older women often do most of this work, although cultural norms in some countries affect women's mobility. The amount of time allocated to these activities is influenced by seasonal patterns of agricultural activity, the availability of substitute goods and services, and environmental changes. A study in Nepal, for instance, found that deforestation associated with a 75 percent rise in the time per trip would increase the time spent gathering fuelwood by 45 percent for all adults and by 50–60 percent for women.[4]

In addition to fuel and water collection, child care is another activity that dominates women's time—although, considering the importance of children to future household welfare, the amount of direct time spent with children is limited. The seven-country study suggests that more time is spent on child care in female-headed households. Female-headed households tend to have high dependency ratios and relatively large numbers of children, implying more child-care time overall, but not necessarily on a per child basis. (Kumar and Hotchkiss 1988).

When a large proportion of women's use of time goes unrecorded, the design of projects and policies can yield false evaluations of costs and benefits. For example, women's unpaid work may be assumed to have zero value. As a result, women's response to changing incentives may be predicted as being higher than their time constraints actually allow. Project benefits—such as the time saved by locating piped water close to homes or by expanding rural electrification—may also be undervalued. Conversely, the benefits of freeing up time may be far more significant than might have been thought. A study in Tanzania, for example, shows that relieving certain time constraints in a community of smallholder coffee and banana growers increases household cash incomes by 10 percent, labor productivity by 15 percent, and capital productivity by 44 percent (Tibaijuka 1994).

Formal Sector Employment

Unpaid work and family responsibilities, as well as lack of investment in women's education, are strongly associated with women's relatively low rates of participation and their limited earnings in formal sector labor markets. Women's participation rates usually dip in the childbearing years, and earnings tend to decline following an interruption in employment. Younger women, on average, work more hours than older women, and married women with young children tend to work less than childless women and mothers of grown children. The correlation of marriage and childrearing with labor market outcomes can be seen even in industrial countries, where wage differences between married women and men are larger than those between single women and men.[5] Similarly, in some developing countries relative earnings decline with age (table 2.2).

When a large proportion of women's use of time goes unrecorded, the design of projects and policies can yield false evaluations of costs and benefits.

Children are not the only reason for interruptions in women's labor force participation; caring for ill or aged family members is often a woman's

In Sample Countries, Single Women Earn More Than Married Women and Younger Women More Than Older Women.

TABLE 2.2   FEMALE-MALE EARNINGS (ADJUSTED FOR HOURS WORKED) BY MARITAL STATUS AND AGE
(percent)

Country	Female-male earnings ratio	
By marital status	*Married*	*Single*
Australia	69	91
Austria	66	97
Germany	57	103
Norway	72	92
Sweden	72	94
Switzerland	58	94
United Kingdom	60	95
United States	59	96
By age	*Age 25*	*Age 45*
Brazil	75	63
Colombia	94	70
Indonesia	81	60
Malaysia	82	61
Venezuela	92	70

Sources: Blau and Kahn 1992; Sedlacek, Gutierrez, and Mohindra 1993.

responsibility. A study from Hungary estimates that half of all absenteeism by women workers is the direct result of the need to care for sick relatives (Einhorn 1993).

Thus, women's labor market outcomes can be substantially poorer than those of men because women's employment opportunities are constrained by social arrangements at the family or household level. These social demands are reinforced by legal conventions. Within the labor market itself, social or employer discrimination can affect women and men differently, and these differences are reflected in the resource allocation decisions taken within the household. Although wage discrimination is illegal in many countries, employers may respond to an increase in the supply of workers by segregating jobs by gender or offering less training to women, who they perceive as being temporarily attached to the labor force (even if in fact most women never drop out). For example, women in the former Soviet Union are fairly well educated and have high labor force participation, but they are concentrated in occupations requiring fewer skills and less vocational training than men, and, on average, they earn less than men (Fong 1993).

Female Wages Are Lower than Male Wages, but This Is Changing.

TABLE 2.3   FEMALE-MALE EARNINGS RATIO OVER TIME

Country	*Female-male earnings ratio (percent)*		
	First observation	*Second observation*	*Average annual percentage change*
Brazil	50.2 (1981)	53.6 (1990)	0.7
Colombia	67.2 (1984)	70.2 (1990)	0.7
Côte d'Ivoire	75.7 (1985)	81.4 (1988)	2.4
Indonesia	55.6 (1986)	60.0 (1992)	1.3
Philippines	70.9 (1978)	80.0 (1988)	1.2
Thailand	73.5 (1980)	79.8 (1990)	0.8

Note: Monthly earnings; for Indonesia and Thailand, rural and urban; for all others, urban only.
Source: Tzannatos 1995.

Women's earnings relative to men's tend to increase over time. A study of six developing countries shows that female earnings relative to male earnings increased by 1 percent a year in the 1980s (table 2.3). There were two reasons for this increase: over the years women entered higher-paying sectors, and within sectors, their pay increased in relation to that of men. This gain would have been even greater had it not been for the effect on wages of increased female participation in the labor force. However, the most visible dimension of gender inequality in the formal labor sector remains the wage difference between men and women. Women's wages are, on average, lower than those of men by about 30 to 40 percent.

Social or employer discrimination can affect women and men differently and these differences are reflected in the resource allocation decisions taken within the household.

A recent study of the gender wage gap in Russia shows that after controlling for education differences, the ratio of women's to men's average hourly earnings stands at just over 71 percent; it has remained at that level since the 1960s. Part of the reason for women's lower hourly earnings in Russia and many other countries lies in patterns of occupational segmentation by gender. Some analysts argue that women—who do most of the household work in Russian households and also have high participation in the formal labor market—cope with the burdens imposed on them by taking less demanding work and devoting less time to advancing their careers (Newell and Reilly 1994).

Informal Sector Employment

One difficulty analysts face in interpreting trends in women's labor force participation and employment in developing economies is the large number of women engaged in informal sector activities, many of which overlap with subsistence-oriented household or community-based activities. Informal sector employment in most developing countries, whether in microenterprises or in casual work, is an important source of livelihood for women and their households.

The competitiveness of women's informal sector activities is constrained by women's limited mobility and lack of access to financial and public services.

A recent study in Mexico estimates that 41 percent of the work force in Mexico's major cities is employed in the informal sector (World Bank 1995c). Data from a 1989 survey show that 60 percent of men working in the sector are salaried workers, compared with only 18 percent of women. By contrast, 80 percent of women working in the sector are unpaid family members, as against 37 percent of men. By far the most common activity in the informal sector is commerce (fixed-location or itinerant), followed by repair work, food preparation and sales, and small-scale manufacturing. The sectoral distribution of informal employment reflects the key role informal workers play in supplying goods and services to low-income consumers. Women tend to be concentrated in commerce and men in services and manufacturing, although the percentage differences are relatively small.[6] Two generalizations can be made on the basis of this study: informal sector workers earn less than workers in large firms, and women earn less than men.

Another recent study of four communities in Lusaka, Guayaquil (Ecuador), Metro Manila, and Budapest shows that informal sector activities are especially important for women during periods of economic reform. Although the numbers both of men and of women in the labor force tend to increase during these times, women rely more on the informal sector than men do. The competitiveness of women's informal sector activities is constrained by women's limited mobility and lack of access to financial and public services. Women also tend to specialize in nontraded goods and services that show relatively low average returns to labor. Across the four cities in the study, women earn between 46 and 68 percent of men's wages (Moser 1994).

The ability of informal sector workers to increase their returns depends on access to physical and human capital and their relationship to the institutional and regulatory environment. Contrary to the common belief, many microenterprises face considerable costs associated with the regulatory environment, including registration and licensing fees, as well as outlays for contracts with public authorities concerning zoning regulations and use of public utilities. In Argentina regulatory costs are estimated to absorb as much as 21 percent of the average microfirm's operational expenses. In some sectors, such as manufacturing and construction, the costs of regulation are about 44 percent (World Bank 1994d). In Mexico real regulatory costs, including the costs of compliance and evasion, are about 20 percent of total costs.

Regulatory costs also inhibit job creation in the informal sector. In Argentina across-the-board deregulation could generate as many as 170,000 jobs in small-scale manufacturing alone. Furthermore, poor workers in family-based firms or microenterprises—and particularly women entrepreneurs—often lack access to such basics as water and power. Targeting infrastructure investments to the poor, which takes account of the needs of women entrepreneurs, can significantly enhance their productivity and earnings.

In rural areas, where formal markets often are not well developed, informal employment activities play a vital role. In Asia the proportion of female rural wage laborers increased sharply in the 1960s and 1970s. In India women make up a larger proportion of rural wage laborers than of the entire labor force, probably because of growing landlessness and poverty among rural households. Rural household labor accounts for a disproportionately large share of employment among the poor and an even larger share among women. Furthermore, a larger proportion of female than male laborers are hired on a casual basis, largely because family arrangements, especially lack of control over property, limit women's ability to work (Hart 1986; Bardhan 1993). Low status in the labor market is also linked to low female indicators in education, health, and nutrition.

Providing credit directly to women has a positive effect on household and individual welfare and improved gender equality.

Social norms affecting decisions within the family about occupational choices or migration can also lead to differential patterns of male and female earnings in informal markets (Binswanger and Rosenzweig 1984). Family responsibilities hinder women's geographic mobility, constraining their ability to command high wages and limiting them to certain areas or industries. The concentration of women in certain sectors, especially nontraded goods and services, intensifies competition between women entrepreneurs and wage workers and lowers the returns to female labor. These effects are compounded by women's lack of access to credit, training, and technology.

Gender Inequality in Access to Assets and Services

Access to Financial Markets

The availability of financial services and access to them are considered important for several reasons. First, savings provide a kind of self-insurance. Second, credit helps households maintain a certain level of consumption at those times when their income fluctuates temporarily. Third, credit can be used to fund investments in capital or other inputs that will yield relatively high returns to production, if households cannot finance such investments from their own savings. A fourth and no less important reason is the role of savings and credit in increasing household members' options outside the home.

Inequalities between women and men in access to financial services—particularly credit—are widely documented. Collateral requirements, high transaction costs, limited mobility and education, and other social and cultural barriers contribute to women's inability to obtain credit (Holt and Ribe 1991). The implications for household efficiency and individual well-being differ, however, depending on whether the household pools its financial resources. If, as the unitary household model assumes, a household pools its resources, the characteristics of individual borrowers are less important than if there is little or no pooling. In the first case, credit resources will be used to meet household needs that have been jointly determined, regardless of who the borrower is. In the second case, the use credit is put to and the needs it then satisfies depend on which household member is borrowing.

A recent study of credit programs in Bangladesh sponsored by the World Bank shows that providing credit directly to women has a positive effect on variables typically associated with household and individual welfare and improved gender equality (Pitt and Khandker 1995). The study looks at three programs in Bangladesh: the Grameen Bank, the Bangladesh Rural Advancement Committee (BRAC), and the Bangladesh Rural Development Board (BRDB). In 1993 women accounted for 94 percent of Grameen Bank members, 82 percent of BRAC members, and 68 percent of BRDB members (Khandker and Khalily 1995; Khandker, Lavy, and Filmer 1994). Only the results for the Grameen Bank are presented here.

Table 2.4 presents the impact of credit obtained by women and men on a variety of social and economic indicators. The results show a clear and positive impact of both male and female borrowing on all indicators of

Loans to Women and Men Have Important Welfare Implications.

TABLE 2.4   WELFARE EFFECTS OF GRAMEEN BANK LOANS
(percentage increase)

Welfare change	Effect of male borrowing	Effect of female borrowing
Increase in boys' schooling	7.2	6.1
Increase in girls' schooling	3.0	4.7
Increase in per capita expenditure	1.8	4.3
Reduction in recent fertility	7.4	3.5
Increase in women's labor supply to cash-income earning activities	0	10.4
Increase in women's nonland assets	0	19.9

Source: Pitt and Khandker 1995.

family welfare, especially through an increase in per capita expenditure, increases in both boys' and girls' schooling, and a reduction in fertility. Female borrowing has a greater effect on girls' schooling and per capita expenditure than does male borrowing; male borrowing has a greater effect on boys' schooling and fertility than does female borrowing. Interestingly, female borrowing also results in more female ownership of nonland assets and an increased supply of female labor to cash-income-earning activities (Pitt and Khandker 1995).

The introduction of programs such as the Grameen Bank in a village has a positive effect on agricultural and nonagricultural production (Khandker and Chowdhury 1994; Rahman and Khandker 1994). The probability that women will be self-employed rather than work for wages increases by 52 percent. The latter finding is important because much of the wage employment open to women in rural areas is very poorly remunerated and can be quite exploitative. Self-employment can bring the opportunity of higher returns for women, plus the freedom to integrate their cash-earning activities into other work as they see fit.

Access to financial services alone cannot reduce gender inequalities in the allocation of household resources. A qualitative study reviewing several targeted credit programs in Bangladesh cautions against overgeneralizing about the benefits of giving women access to credit. The study finds that it is difficult to infer that increased borrowing alone improves women's bargaining power because in many rural Bangladeshi households the question of who controls the resources is quite complex (Goetz and Sen Gupta 1994). Nevertheless, the possibility of receiving credit (or, similarly, of working for wages) may give women greater bargaining power within the household. This bargaining power can be used to improve child health and nutrition and may increase the likelihood that children will attend school.

Access to Land and Property

The ownership of land and the distribution of land rights influence the productivity of labor and capital resources and the incentive to invest in resource management. Private property rights, in particular, are associated with increased access to product and factor markets, especially credit markets, and to public services such as public utilities and agricultural extension. However, relatively little direct evidence exists to link independent ownership of land by women with increased access and productivity. One obstacle to empirical work is that women's access to land and property is often mediated through marriage. (A married woman's land rights are frequently limited to "use" rather than ownership.) Furthermore, complex systems of land tenure make it difficult to generalize about the effects of ownership on productivity. Nonetheless, some evidence suggests that independent land rights for women could enhance both the efficiency with which resources are used and the well-being of women and their households (Agarwal 1994).

> *The possibility of receiving credit may give women greater bargaining power within the household, which can be used to improve child health and nutrition.*

While independent land rights may increase efficiency and household welfare, lack of secure land tenure appears to be associated with low investments by women in land conservation. In Zimbabwe's communal areas, land that a woman acquires is often allocated to her only temporarily; for example, the location of land allotments received from husbands or borrowed from neighbors is usually subject to periodic change (Jackson 1993). The same is true in parts of West Africa (David 1992; Jackson 1993). Uncertainty about the permanence of their control over the land means that women may be reluctant to invest in improvements that will benefit the landowner rather than the user.

A significant trend in recent decades in developing countries has been the move toward private ownership. In some countries, this trend has been encouraged by reforms dealing with land redistribution, tenancy, or land titling. Such reforms are considered important for promoting long-term investments and the adoption of the latest technology. They also provide the collateral people need to gain access to credit and other factor markets. Ironically, evidence also suggests that prereform inequalities in male and female land rights are reinforced by land reform programs. For example, in Latin America most reforms are based on the premise that the man of the household is the household head. This presumption means that women (except for widows and single mothers) have no rights to land ownership. Even where women and men benefit equally from land reform, differences exist between nominal and real land rights (see box 2.3).

In the central part of European Russia and in Moldova the lands and assets of state and collective farms are being parceled out in allotments as part of wider economic reforms. Every person who lived and worked on a collective farm receives a share of the land. Data show that although, on average, women have received a slightly higher proportion of land shares than men, the nonland capital assets of the old farms are being distributed as property shares on the basis of a formula heavily weighted toward an individual's wage rate and years of employment. Such criteria favor men over women and give men more valuable property shares. Dividends paid on these property shares also tend to be higher than those paid on land shares (Holt 1995).

Land reform programs that fail to account for gender differences in rights

---

BOX 2.3 WHO GETS ACCESS TO LAND? HONDURAS AND CAMEROON

Honduras' Agrarian Modernization Law of 1974 includes a provision giving men age 16 or older the right to access to land, independent of any other qualification. For women, however, this right is restricted to unmarried mothers or widows with dependent children. Furthermore, if a male beneficiary dies or becomes incapacitated, the law gives preference in inheritance rights to a male child over the child's legally married mother. Some 30 percent of rural Honduran households are headed by women at least part time because of the seasonal migration of men to look for work (Saito and Spurling 1992).

In the northwest and southwest provinces of Cameroon, an estimated 50 percent or more of those who claimed land within the first ten years of land registration (1974–85) were classified as public servants. Over 32 percent of all the remaining land titles went to businesses.

Women make up more than 51 percent of Cameroon's population and do more than 75 percent of the agricultural work, but they are virtually absent from land registers. Only 3.2 percent of all land titles issued in the Northwest Province were given to women; in the Southwest Province the figure was 7.2 percent. For the country as a whole, it is estimated that women obtained under 10 percent of all land certificates (World Bank 1995a).

to own, use, and transfer land may actually exacerbate the insecurity of women's land claims and, as a result, harm household welfare. For example, there is evidence that land titling focused on male household heads has adversely affected women's ability to farm independently. Moreover, intrahousehold inequalities in income and decisionmaking have increased (FAO 1993). In Africa some titling programs have allowed men to take advantage of their control over land to redesignate land formerly cultivated by women as household land. This switch provided the opportunity for men to increase the amount of work they expect from women on household plots. In other cases women have received smaller and less fertile plots than they had before for their personal crops (FAO 1993).

Recognizing women's independent claims to land is therefore an important issue in property reform. In poor households, having rights to land could alleviate both women's own poverty and the household's risk of remaining poor. The reason is mainly that women's access to economic resources has a positive effect on household welfare (Agarwal 1994). From the point of view of efficiency, secure land tenure increases the incentive to manage resources efficiently and expands access to formal credit markets. Because secure land tenure can mean greater productivity, it may also increase the household's incentives to invest in women's human capital.

Access to Extension Services

Agricultural extension services provide information, training, and technology to agricultural producers. Extension services have always been regarded as necessary for agricultural modernization. Given the importance of women's labor to agriculture in most regions, providing women with access to agricultural extension services is essential for current and future productivity. Types of agricultural extension services vary, but in most countries publicly provided services dominate. Evidence suggests that women have not benefited as much as men have from publicly provided extension services.

Given the importance of women's labor to agriculture in most regions, providing women with access to agricultural extension services is essential for current and future productivity.

A review of five African countries shows that extension agents are more likely to visit male farmers than female farmers (table 2.5). The impact of this inequity on female productivity depends in part on whether women and men within households pool information. There is, however, little evidence

Female-Headed Households Receive Fewer Extension Services.

TABLE 2.5   VISITS BY AGRICULTURAL EXTENSION AGENTS
(percentage of households visited)

Country and year	Households with male head	Households with female head
Kenya, 1989	12	9
Malawi, 1989	70	58
Nigeria, 1989	37	22
Tanzania, 1984	40	20
Zambia		
1982	57	29
1986	60	19

Source: Quisumbing 1994.

to suggest that this happens (see box 2.4). It is important to ensure that extension services reach women directly, not only to redress gender inequalities but also to maximize productive efficiency. Women play a critical role in production of food and cash crops for the household, in postharvest activities, and in livestock care. Men and women perform different tasks; they can substitute for one another only to a limited extent, and this limitation creates different demands for extension information. Also, as men leave farms in search of paid employment in urban areas, women are increasingly managing and operating farms on a regular and full-time basis. Hence, women are becoming a constituency for extension and research services in their own right (World Bank 1994e).

BOX 2.4 DO WOMEN FARMERS LEARN FROM THEIR HUSBANDS?

A survey of women farmers in Burkina Faso found that 40 percent had some knowledge of modern crop and livestock production technologies. For most of these women, relatives and friends were the source of information; nearly one-third had acquired their knowledge from the extension service, and only 1 percent had heard of the technologies from their husbands.

Men are less likely to pass information on to their wives when crops and tasks are gender specific. In Malawi women claimed that their husbands rarely passed on advice to them; if their husbands did tell them something, the women did not find it relevant to their needs. In India women learned from friends, relatives, neighbors, and sometimes from their husbands, but this second-hand information seldom changed their production patterns (Saito and Spurling 1992).

The expansion of agricultural services beyond the public sector is a growing phenomenon in developing economies. The inadequacies of public funding, plus the need to provide more client-oriented services, suggest that the private sector has an important role to play. However, women's limited access to land and credit put the many potential benefits offered by extension services out of reach. For example, in Kenya's Meru and Maranga areas more than half the women surveyed cited a shortage of cash as their reason for not adopting technologies that would maximize their output and increase their efficiency. The amount of education women receive and the efficiency with which they run their farms are also closely linked. This tie is particularly significant in light of the fact that one purpose of extension services is to advise farmers on use of modern technology.

Three studies of Kenya found that the gender of the farm manager was, by itself, an insignificant factor in output per hectare but that the manager's educational level had a significant effect on farm productivity (Moock 1976; Saito and Spurling 1992; Bindlish and Evenson 1993). Simulations based on these studies suggest that significant gains could accrue to increased investment in women's physical and human capital. As the data in table 2.6 show,

Increasing Human Capital and Input Levels Would Increase the Yield for Women Farmers.

TABLE 2.6   EFFECTS OF INCREASING WOMEN FARMERS' HUMAN CAPITAL AND INPUT LEVELS

Policy experiment	Increase in yields (percent)
Maize farmers, Kenya, 1976[a]	
Effects of giving female farmers sample mean characteristics and input levels	7
Effects of giving female farmer's men's education and input levels	9
Effects of giving women primary schooling	24
Foodcrop (maize, beans, and cowpeas) farmers, Kenya, 1990[b]	
Effects of giving female farmer men's education and input levels	22.0
Effects of increasing land area to male farmers' levels	10.5
Effects of increasing fertilizer to male farmers' levels	1.6

Note: For simplicity, the assumption was made that changes in one input do not affect others.
a. Coefficients from Moock 1976.
b. Coefficients from Saito and Spurling 1992.

if women and men shared the same educational characteristics and input levels, farm-specific yields would increase between 7 and 22 percent. Giving women primary schooling, by itself, would increase yields by 24 percent. Thus, underinvestment in women's education limits growth of agricultural productivity. Well-targeted extension services can help to narrow the differences in productivity that arise from educational inequalities (Schultz 1988).

Conclusion

Analysts must look beyond market outcomes to identify the sources of persistent inequality between women and men. The search must focus on the household and its role in the formation of present and future human capital and on institutions beyond the household that reinforce and perpetuate gender inequalities. Gender inequalities within the household affect market outcomes, and these feed back into household decisionmaking. This process is reinforced by inequalities in access to assets and services beyond the household. Improving the relative status of women within the household and increasing their access to assets and services will increase the returns to investment in human resources and improve the prospects for sustainable economic growth.

We must look for that
which we have been trained
not to see.

Ann Scales, *Yale Law Journal,* 1986

Public Policies Matter

AS CHAPTER 2 has shown, underinvesting in girls and women is inefficient for society as a whole. Correcting for past underinvestment will require a "gendered" approach to public policy. How this can be concretely achieved is the topic of this chapter.

Equalizing Opportunities by Modifying the Legal Framework

Laws form the functional framework of the economy and of civil society. Equality in the legal treatment of men and women creates the legitimacy policymakers need to seek change. Legal and regulatory provisions that discriminate against women—that, for example, bar married women from seeking employment or prevent women from holding legal title to land— perpetuate gender inequalities and severely restrict women's ability to participate fully in social and economic development.

Modifying the legal framework to eliminate discrimination and equalize opportunities for women and men is an important goal for public policy at the national and international levels. A supportive legal environment is also vital for other aspects of public policy that have a direct bearing on the opportunities available to women, such as regulations affecting the formal and informal sectors.

Four areas of the law are particularly important for equalizing the opportunities available to men and women: land and property rights; labor market policies and employment law; family law; and financial laws and regulations.

Land and Property Rights

Policymakers should ensure that women and men are treated equally in the public allocation of land. Eligibility for land reform programs, for example, should not discriminate against women's prereform claims, whether the women are heads of households or members of households headed by men. When communities have been resettled or when a project allocates land to participating producers, women should have the same rights to land as men. For instance, refugee and displaced women returning to their homelands, often as de facto heads of households, need fair and equal treatment to allow them to establish a farming or enterprise base as soon as possible. Where land is in short supply, it may be necessary to recognize the land rights of certain groups, as well as their individual rights. The Indian National Sericulture Project is an example; it has leased land to women's groups and promoted women's access to land under state land-grant schemes (Quisumbing 1994).

Some countries have enacted legislation to ensure gender equality in property and contractual rights. Under China's Law of Succession, for example, males and females have equal rights to inheritance. Complementary measures are needed to ensure that women know their rights. Such measures include "legal literacy" programs and campaigns to make judges and administrators sensitive to gender issues in the area of property rights (see box 3.1).

Labor Market Policies and Employment Law

Discriminatory labor market policies and employment laws are widespread; examples are bans on hiring married women and restrictions on the type of work pregnant women may perform. Labor laws may also restrict female participation in jobs and deny women access to work settings. Even legislation that seeks to promote equal opportunity can have unintended outcomes for women workers. For example, generous maternity and child-care benefits for women workers may make hiring women relatively more costly than hiring men, perpetuating the gender wage gap.

The main issue for public policy is to ensure that fair and equal employment laws exist and are enforced.

BOX 3.1 SOME NGO EFFORTS TO
PROMOTE WOMEN'S LEGAL LITERACY

Schuler and Kadirgamar-Rajasingham (1992) describe innovative approaches by nongovernmental organizations to provide women with useful legal knowledge and tools.

The Caribbean Association for Feminist Research and Action (CAFRA) has launched "women and the law" projects in five English-speaking Caribbean countries. Using a participatory methodology, the projects aim to create awareness of the law, provide women with legal information that will be useful to them in their daily lives, identify specific areas for action, and influence overall legislative policy. The projects develop educational materials for legal literacy and offer topic-specific paralegal training for women's organizations.

The legal literacy program of the Ugandan Women Lawyers' Association (FIDA-Uganda) conducts legal literacy campaigns on specified dates each month in different districts. Pairs of FIDA volunteers conduct sessions, using role playing and discussions, on legal topics of relevance to women's lives and provide advice on contacting the FIDA legal clinic for advice and representation. In addition, FIDA and Action for Development broadcast regular radio and television programs on women and the law and publish pamphlets on legal issues of interest to women.

In India the Self-Employed Women's Association (SEWA) holds worker education meetings to provide members with legal information and offers one-day training sessions on specialized legal information for community leaders. Members of SEWA paralegal staff research cases, prepare briefs, and argue all cases in labor courts for members. SEWA's legal literacy efforts are part of its overall strategy of action for supporting self-employed women and women in the informal sector.

In this regard, the main issue for public policy is to ensure that fair and equal employment laws exist and are enforced. Such laws should cover employment and employment-related benefits and should not be applied in a way that restricts women's access to the labor market.

In many countries women are protected by special standards in the workplace. These safeguards are of two types. The first includes measures intended to end discrimination in the labor market by requiring equal pay for work of equal value or by prohibiting the exclusion of workers from certain jobs because of gender. The second type protects women in their role as mothers by requiring employers to pay the full cost of maternity leave and provide childcare facilities, restricting night work, and limiting work categorized as dangerous or hazardous.

The first type of labor standard is often difficult to enforce, although nearly 120 countries have enacted equal opportunity laws. In most cases the law is in place but is not enforced. Furthermore, it often applies only to the formal sector of the labor market, leaving large numbers of women in the informal sector with little protection. More concerted public and private action is required to devise appropriate mechanisms for enforcement. In addition, complementary measures are needed to increase women's chances of entering the labor force. Such measures would include more merit-based hiring of women in the public sector and the creation of an appropriate regulatory framework that encourages the establishment of day-care centers, private nursery schools, and kindergartens for the children of workers in both the formal and informal sectors. (Box 3.2 describes a day-care project in Bolivia.)

Many countries have laws that limit night work, overtime, and the use of heavy machinery by women. While well intentioned, these laws, too, can reduce women's employment options by raising the employer's cost of hiring women and perpetuating the notion that women workers are less flexible than male workers. This adverse result occurs because women already tend to have lower levels of human capital than men and are limited by traditional notions of what constitutes "appropriate" women's work. Devising effective protective legislation for women is thus a difficult balancing act.

Effective laws to protect women must honor the fine line between ensuring safe working conditions for all workers, including women in the informal sector, and providing equal opportunities for all workers seeking employment. Standards relating to maternity leave and child-care benefits are common in the formal sector. To ensure that such standards do not raise the costs of female labor unnecessarily, employment legislation should avoid having employers pay benefits directly. Maternity benefits should be funded through general revenue taxes

---

BOX 3.2 DAY-CARE CENTERS IN BOLIVIA

As in other Latin American countries, women in Bolivia are overrepresented among the poor, and many live in difficult circumstances. They are twice as likely as men to be illiterate, their access to child care is limited, they are subject to discrimination in hiring and wages, and they are restricted by law from engaging in certain productive activities.

The Integrated Child Development Project, financed by a credit from the World Bank's International Development Association (IDA), is designed to enhance the status of women by increasing their employment opportunities and their knowledge of education, health, and nutrition. The project will establish day-care centers to provide nonformal, home-based, integrated child development for children under the age of 6 in thirty-four poor urban and periurban areas. Women benefit from the project either as caregivers employed at the minimum wage or as clients of the centers. Placing children in day care gives women more time to search for jobs or to improve their current situations (Winkler and Guedes 1995).

or social security systems rather than by direct contributions from individual employers. In Eastern Europe and Latin America, however, this method of funding benefits has imposed a significant cost on the treasury, raising the question of how much should be paid and for how long.

One way of addressing this issue is for governments to encourage women and men to share the responsibility for childrearing by adopting legislation allowing either parent to qualify for the leave and benefits associated with having a child (Folbre 1994). Such legislation can be supported by changes in the tax system to ensure equal treatment of workers within the household and a marginal tax rate on the earnings of additional workers in the household low enough to avoid creating a disincentive to women's participation in the labor force (MacDonald 1994). These tax changes can be complemented by legislation that encourages absent fathers to pay child support. Such laws are in place in many Latin American and Caribbean countries, but none systematically monitors transfers (Folbre 1994). Greater efforts to enforce the law are needed.

Family Law

Gender inequality in family law can worsen women's bargaining position within and outside the household and affect household welfare and efficiency. As noted in chapter 2, women's bargaining position in relation to household resource allocation is often a key factor in determining the well-being of household members, particularly children. Reforms of family law can enhance women's economic and social opportunities while still respecting cultural norms. For instance, the minimum age of marriage for women should be set high enough so that girls can complete secondary schooling; this would help lower fertility rates. (Allowing for exceptions such as parental consent negates the potential fertility benefit.) Marriage contracts should include stipulations guaranteeing the wife's rights, especially on separation.

Women's bargaining position in relation to household resource allocation is often a key factor in determining the well-being of household members, particularly children.

Legal and policy measures can have a direct bearing on the health of women. The law and its enforcement are essential for combating domestic violence against women. If the laws on violence against women are to be enforced, women need to be made aware of the legal recourse available to them, and the judiciary and police need to be sensitized to the existence and

Brazil's women-only police stations
are an innovative approach to the
problem of violence against women.
They have been so successful that
other countries—including Argentina,
Colombia, Costa Rica, India, Peru,
and Uruguay—have emulated them.
The police stations have made it
easier for women to report gender-
based crimes of violence, and, with
that experience, women are now demanding more support from the police, such as legal counseling and
advice. Despite the program's success, the number of convictions for
gender-based crimes has not increased, largely because similar in-
novations have not been made in the
judicial system (Heise, Pitanguy, and
Germain 1994).

In Zimbabwe the Mussasa project
provides support and counseling to
abused women and sensitizes police
and prosecutors to the issues of domestic violence and rape. To ensure
the credibility and acceptability of the
training, legal professionals are involved in the program. One branch of
the criminal justice system—the police department, for example—often
hosts training for another, such as
prosecutors (Stewart 1992).

In Costa Rica El Instituto Legal de
las Naciones Unidas y Desarrollo runs
gender sensitization training for prosecutors, judges, lawyers, and other
professionals who deal with crimes of
violence against women (Heise,
Pitanguy, and Germain 1994).

implications of violence against women. Affirmative action policies can
increase the number of women police officers, lawyers, and judges. Training
police, lawyers, and judges can increase their gender sensitivity, making the
legal system more responsive to women's needs. Legal literacy efforts can
make women aware of their rights and show them how to use these rights to
mobilize for change. Some approaches to dealing with domestic violence are
illustrated in box 3.3.

Financial Laws and Regulations

Access to credit is vital for women, allowing them to manage fluctuations in
income and expenditures and to expand their businesses. As we saw in the
preceding chapters, credit can be an important source of economic empowerment for women within the household. But in many countries, underdeveloped
financial markets, controlled interest rates, and overly rigid banking regulations
have led to systems of credit rationing that tend to shut out the poor, many of
whom are women. If financial institutions are to lend to those unable to obtain
credit in the current environment, interest rates must be liberalized. Positive
interest rates have important effects on informal money markets, which tend to
be more exploitative when formal sector credit is rationed.[7]

Changes in the laws governing access to credit are also vital because women's business profiles often differ from men's. Compared with men, women are more likely to work in low-risk, small, and home-based businesses (Rhyne and Holt 1994). This situation creates a demand for small loans that can be obtained without formal, legally secured collateral and that offer relatively flexible repayment terms. Legislation that encourages broad access to financial institutions can increase the availability of these types of loans, but legal changes may also be needed to extend the range of acceptable collateral.

In many countries the regulatory framework contains provisions that are especially punitive to small firms. This adds an additional constraint on women, whose businesses are concentrated at the small end of the size spectrum. The deregulation of the microenterprise sector would remove implicit disincentives to small-firm activity and would relieve some of these constraints. Such action would enhance women entrepreneurs' prospects of benefiting from training or credit programs targeted to the microenterprise sector (World Bank 1994d, 1995c).

Redirecting Public Policies and Expenditure to Promote Gender Equality

It is unlikely that legal reform by itself will be sufficient to ensure that women and men are treated equally. Further public action may be required to guarantee that gender-neutral laws are enforced at both national and local levels.

Macroeconomic Policies

Many developing countries are implementing important policy and institutional reforms to address changing economic conditions on both the domestic and international fronts. These reforms are often supported by international financial institutions and bilateral donors. The pace of reform has varied across countries. Those countries that have implemented reforms early on, carried them out consistently, and received adequate financial support have generally enjoyed faster and stronger economic growth than countries that have undertaken reforms too slowly, too intermittently, or not at all. Where implementation has been slow or the government's commitment weak, economic distortions have tended to multiply and economic growth to slow, limiting the government's ability to invest in physical and human capital for the future.

It is often the poorest groups in society that stand to lose the most from economic distortions. High and rising inflation places a disproportionate tax burden on the poor, including low-paid wage workers and those with fixed incomes. For this and other reasons, inflation tends to hit women harder than men. An overvalued currency is also regressive; it keeps the price of imported goods artificially low, crowding out many locally produced goods. Women's businesses, which are often concentrated in the informal sector, can be particularly vulnerable to competition from cheap imports. An overvalued currency reduces international competitiveness, limiting the availability of foreign exchange for domestic entrepreneurs and constraining business expansion and employment creation. A firm commitment to policy reform is therefore essential to economic growth and sustainable initiatives for alleviating poverty.

Inflation tends to hit women harder than men.

Such reforms generally include two kinds of necessary policies. The first emphasizes macroeconomic stability and the removal of price distortions; the second promotes labor-demanding growth in agriculture and industry and better, more accessible basic social services, mainly in education, health care, and water supply. Macroeconomic stability can be achieved by reducing large current account and government budget deficits and by curtailing excessive money and credit expansion. Correct pricing of foreign exchange and of domestic goods and services facilitates trade and investment and promotes growth. Reforms of trade and price incentives encourage job creation and higher earnings.

In short, broadly based economic reforms benefit the poor, as the experiences of diverse countries have shown. Data from the LSMS and similar studies confirm that in Costa Rica, Ethiopia, Ghana, Indonesia, Peru, the Philippines, and Tanzania, declines in poverty rates have accompanied economic reforms. Because of underlying gender inequalities, reductions in poverty do not necessarily improve the economic status of women. Nonetheless, although empirical evidence on changes in women's welfare following reforms is scarce, data from the Philippines suggest that for women, economic reform is accompanied by improvements in social indicators and important employment gains (box 3.4). An analysis of household data from Peru indicates that reforms there have not only led to renewed growth and reduced poverty but have also improved the status of female-headed households (box 3.5).

Despite their seminal role in encouraging sustainable, long-term growth, some economic reforms involve transitional costs, for two reasons: the need to implement radical shifts in government policy, and the lag, perhaps of years, between acceleration of economic growth and the realization of the

BOX 3.4 SOCIAL PROGRESS AND LABOR FORCE GAINS FOR WOMEN IN THE PHILIPPINES

The Philippines began implementing economic reforms in the early 1980s. While political turmoil and some policy slippage have weakened GDP growth over the period and led to the need for further reforms, quality of life indicators have improved during adjustment. For example, by 1990 the incidence of absolute poverty had declined by about one-third (to approximately 20 percent of the population). Maternal and infant mortality rates also declined over the period: in 1980 the infant mortality rate was 52 per 1,000 live births, but by 1990 it had fallen to 41 per 1,000 births (Johansen 1993).

The percentage of the population with access to safe drinking water increased between 1980 and 1990, from 65 to 93 percent of the urban population and from 43 to 72 percent of the rural population. The figures for sanitation services showed the same increase, climbing from 81 percent with access in 1980 to 98 per-

cent in 1990 among urban dwellers and from 67 to 85 percent among those in rural areas. Secondary school enrollment rates for boys and girls also showed gains. Girls and boys have traditionally reached similar educational levels in the Philippines, a trend that contributed to women's gains in the labor market during adjustment in the 1980s. While labor force participation rates for men rose only slightly, the rates for women increased dramatically, from 23 to 37 percent.

At the same time, women's wages as a percentage of men's grew from 71 to 80 percent between 1978 and 1988 (Tzannatos 1995). A recent study of a low-income community in Manila found that in some private sector jobs women earn more than men, reflecting in part the high educational level among women in the sector. Earnings in the informal sector are generally low for both women and men, although some women have been so successful in their informal sector businesses that their spouses have opted to leave low-paying jobs in the formal sector to participate in their wives' enterprises (Moser 1994).

benefits of growth by large segments of the population. The short-term costs can include increases in food prices as subsidies are removed, temporary restrictions on credit to control monetary expansion, and cuts in public spending as governments attempt to control budget deficits and reorient spending toward the most important public services. Moreover, inequalities in access to and control over resources and in entry into markets hamper some groups in taking advantage of the opportunities created by economic reform. For example, people who are unable to acquire new skills may remain unemployed for some time. Gender inequalities in access to and control over land in rural areas can keep women farmers from taking advantage of changes in the relative prices of tradable and nontradable crops.

BOX 3.5 MACROECONOMIC REFORM AND IMPROVED LIVING STANDARDS IN PERU

Between 1985 and 1990 Peru's economic regime was marked by expansionary monetary and fiscal policies and high levels of government intervention in most areas of the economy. Although these policies led to an initial period of growth, the approach proved unsustainable; by late 1987 growth had given way to hyperinflation and deep recession. During 1988–90 real GDP dropped by an average of 8 percent a year. Real wages and consumption expenditure also fell sharply as inflation soared to 7,600 percent a year in 1990.

In 1990 the new government of President Alberto Fujimori introduced macroeconomic reform measures designed to stabilize the economy, reduce fiscal deficits and inflation, increase market efficiency, and improve the country's competitiveness. Under this reform program inflation declined dramatically, falling to 57 percent in 1992 and to 17 percent in 1994. Real GDP grew by about 20 percent between 1991 and 1994, while real per capita consumption ex-penditure grew by more than 18.5 percent. LSMS data show that poverty declined by 11 percent—from 55 percent of the population in 1991 to 49 percent in 1994. Although the country experienced a brief contractionary period following the introduction of reform measures, household data from Lima for 1990, 1991, and 1994 indicate that in 1994 per capita expenditure was well above, and the incidence of poverty well below, 1990 levels.

Improvements in living standards have been widespread, and the largest gains have been made in some of the country's poorest regions, such as the urban and rural *sierra* (mountain areas). In most parts of the country, increases in per capita expenditure among households headed by women have been above the national average. In the urban and rural *sierra,* for example, consumption expenditure by these households increased by 47.7 and 44.8 percent, respectively—figures that compare favorably with increases in per capita expenditure among households headed by men (35 and 28 percent for the same regions).

Although both women and men are expected to gain from economic reform in the long run, gender inequalities at the household and market levels can mean that the benefits of reform reach women, especially poor women, only slowly. Reforms must incorporate measures aimed at counteracting short-term transitional costs. Among the most important are safety nets specifically targeted to vulnerable groups. For example, in fiscal 1994 seventeen of the twenty-three reform programs supported by the World Bank included components aimed specifically at reducing poverty; fourteen of them supported targeted programs or safety net measures such as labor-intensive public works projects, targeted nutrition and social assistance programs, and unemployment and social security schemes (see box 3.6).

BOX 3.6 FOOD COUPONS IMPROVE NUTRITION IN HONDURAS

The food coupon program in Honduras, part of a social safety net supported by the World Bank and financed by IDA and other donors, was put in place in 1990 to protect the country's most vulnerable people during economic reforms. Starting with about 182,000 participants, by 1994 the program had expanded its coverage to 345,000 of the estimated 430,000 children at risk of malnutrition. The effort also supports nutrition education for health workers, community groups, and mothers. Because coupons are used instead of food, the government saves some 30 percent over traditional food distribution costs, and the beneficiaries are able to choose the food they will consume. Beginning in 1995, an adjustment for inflation will maintain the value of the coupons, enabling participants to satisfy a constant proportion of their food needs.

The project also supports the development and implementation of a long-term nutrition assistance strategy for Honduras. Although attempting to measure changes in malnutrition is difficult in the short term, there have already been noticeable benefits. Between 1990 and 1993 the number of first-graders with severe or moderate malnutrition dropped by 4 percent. Organizers are now trying to graduate women participants from the program by offering training in basic skills such as food processing and helping them find assembly work in local factories (World Bank 1995b).

However, safety nets are not a substitute for a more integrated approach to economic and social policy that includes appropriate levels of investment in social services and infrastructure. Recognizing this fact, governments and donors are increasingly incorporating into their reform packages antipoverty initiatives and measures to reduce gender inequality. In Pakistan, for example, the IDA-financed Public Sector Adjustment Program provides much-needed financial support for the balance of payments account and reinforces the emphasis on government investment in the social sectors. The program promotes increased access to and improvements in basic education, health, and water supply services that benefit girls and women in rural areas. It also supports a shift in government education and health spending toward the primary level.

Although both women and men are expected to gain from economic reform in the long run, gender inequalities at the household and market levels can mean that the benefits of reform reach women, especially poor women, only slowly.

In fiscal 1994 twelve of twenty-three World Bank economic reform programs emphasized the restructuring of public expenditures, primarily to maintain and increase spending on education, health care, and other areas important to poverty reduction, such as water supply and sanitation. The Burkina
Faso reform program is typical; it supports an increase in the total budgeted
amounts for primary education and health services, which are particularly
beneficial to the poor and to women. Uganda's program seeks to protect and
enhance public expenditures for basic social services, including water supply, primary health care, and primary education. In the long term, the reform
of public spending—especially in the social sectors, physical infrastructure,
and agricultural research and extension—promises significant benefits for
women.

Sectoral Investments

In principle, public expenditures on social services and infrastructure are
allocated on a gender-neutral basis; in practice, men and women use these
services differently. The resulting inequalities frequently perpetuate gender-
based differences in the accumulation and distribution of human capital
within households. Public policy can address this problem by rearranging
public expenditure priorities between sectors and within social sectors. Furthermore, it can support services and types of infrastructure that provide the
highest social returns to public spending and are most heavily used by women
and children.

EDUCATION. Estimations of the private returns to education for a number
of countries (Psacharopoulos 1994) show that returns are at least equal for
girls and boys and are often higher for girls. Moreover, these rates do not
capture the externalities generated by providing education to girls. The com-
bination of private and social returns provides a clear signal for restructuring
the allocation of public resources so as to support female education. Yet
incidence analysis for a number of countries for which the necessary data are
available reveals that educational subsidies per capita are higher for males
than for females. This difference is partly a result of the bias in allocation of
subsidies toward higher levels of education, where female enrollment is
lowest. Distortions in the allocation of public resources, such as the provision
of more money for male-dominated tertiary institutions than for education
that benefits girls, should be corrected by reallocating spending toward basic
(primary and lower-secondary) schooling. Targeting these educational levels
will have the maximum effect on girls' education and will yield higher social
returns for society as a whole. In countries where universal basic education
has been achieved and capital markets are unable to help households finance

higher education, continuing to subsidize higher education may be warranted. The rationale for the subsidy would be the productivity gains associated with a better-trained labor force.

To correct the bias against enrollment of girls, more targeted interventions are needed to influence household decisionmaking.

However, reallocating public spending toward primary education and later toward higher levels is not sufficient to erase the gender gap in education. The bias against enrolling girls in school is evident in both poor and nonpoor households and applies even at the primary level. To correct this bias, more targeted interventions are needed to influence household decisionmaking.

HEALTH. Correcting the gender bias in the public financing of health care is a more complex process than correcting the bias in education, for two main reasons: the marked differences between the health needs of men and women, and the unreliability of household data on demand for health services (in comparison with the data on demand for education). However, it is clear that targeting health services to women implies provision of adequate funding for perinatal care, infant immunization, and mother and child health services. Because of the significant social benefits of providing women with appropriate health care, governments should make basic services that benefit women a top priority among public health care expenditures.

There is a critical link between the public provision of health care and women's access to educational opportunities. A mother educated to seek preventive care and early treatment of illness for herself and her children (particularly girls) will reduce the cost of health care and, in many cases, prevent premature death. Most of these highly cost-effective services can be supplied in rural clinics and health centers. Public spending should be so allocated as to ensure sufficient funding for these primary health facilities.

AGRICULTURAL EXTENSION SERVICES. Agricultural extension and research services are widely considered vital to increasing and sustaining agricultural productivity. Many of these services are being provided by the private sector, but in some countries private services need public support, either because certain markets have not yet been developed or because the infrastructure is poorly developed. However, women farmers and smallholders are often not served as effectively by public agricultural extension systems as are commercial and male farmers (FAO 1993). This disparity stems partly from expenditure priorities within agricultural extension services, which concentrate resources on the crops and the technology controlled primarily by male commercial farmers. Reallocating public spending on agricultural extension and research services toward crops and technology raised by or used by smallholders and women farmers could yield high social returns to public investment and could increase private returns by improving the skills and productivity of small agricultural producers.

Reallocating public spending on agricultural extension and research services toward crops and technology raised by or used by women farmers could yield high social returns to public investment.

Techniques for reaching smallholders and women farmers should take into account the need for quality and cost-effectiveness in public services. Economies of scale can be achieved if extension agents deal with groups of farmers instead of with individuals. This approach also provides a valuable forum for exchanging information, fostering peer learning, sharing expensive equipment, and pooling resources for credit. Mobile training units and flexible hours that fit the crowded schedules of women farmers should also be considered, and more female extension agents should be trained to deal directly with female farmers. Such measures can be introduced without large additional resources if existing expenditures are carefully reallocated.

INFRASTRUCTURE. Public investment in economic and social infrastructure is vital in facilitating individual and household investment in physical and human capital. However, public expenditures on roads, water supply, and sanitation infrastructure frequently do not meet the needs of those who use the services most heavily. Women are the main users of water services, and it is essential to involve them in designing and implementing water projects. For example, in areas where transport is inadequate and water collection is a daily burden for women and children, the population tends to use the closest available facility rather than the safest one. In such cases, projects that ensure a safe water supply and take into account the specific needs and constraints of the users often have a significant effect on users' health. In two villages in Zaire where a piped water network was installed to provide safe drinking water, the median incidence of diarrhea was halved among children in households located less than a five-minute walk from a public standpipe. Spending allocations that favor public water supply and sanitation improve the general health of the population, save time for women and children, and increase school attendance. A study from Morocco shows that access to tap and well water instead of pond or river water raised school enrollment for both boys and girls (Khandker, Lavy, and Filmer 1994).

Women are the main users of water services, and it is essential to involve them in designing and implementing water projects.

Public spending on roads and energy-related facilities (for instance, electrification or energy conservation) or other infrastructure is usually assumed to be gender neutral. Yet women and men use these facilities differently. The Morocco study cited above found that the availability of electricity increased the enrollment rate for girls substantially more than for boys. The study also showed that the presence of a paved road increased by 40 percent the probability that girls would attend school and reduced by 5 percent their probability of dropping out. Overall, improved road conditions increased the probability of school attendance for girls by 32 percent and for boys by 20 percent.

Rural electrification can also ease the time constraints on women who must balance household and productive work. Lack of time is often a primary reason for women's weak response to economic incentives, especially in rural areas. The case for making public investments in infrastructure would be stronger if gender differences in the use of projects and services, as well as the potential effect of such investment on productivity and social development, were taken into account.

Using Targeting Measures to Narrow the Gender Gap

As we have seen, policies that specifically target women or girls can address the needs of this group more efficiently and with greater cost-effectiveness than general policy measures. Female household members tend to allocate resources more directly to children, while men tend to allocate more resources to adults. In households in which resources are not pooled, targeting programs to the household as a whole will not necessarily benefit all members equally.

Targeting women directly is justifiable on two grounds. First, to the extent that gender inequalities prevent an economy from realizing its full potential, targeting to women can be an effective strategy for increasing productivity and output. Second, where gender differences are wide, targeting may be needed to capture social gains and to increase internal efficiency.

BOX 3.7 STRIVING FOR GENDER-NEUTRAL OUTCOMES IN CHINA

In China the introduction of compulsory education laws in 1986 was complemented by policies intended to reduce poverty and increase gender equality. The main decision underlying these policies was to devolve responsibility for primary education to local communities. The communities were expected to devise appropriate measures to raise primary enrollments, especially of girls, taking into account specific local problems. Various measures were developed, including awareness campaigns to motivate parents to enroll all children, flexible work schedules, evening classes, sibling care, and special schools for girls. The strategy succeeded in raising enrollments among both girls and boys, even in some of the poorest and most remote regions (World Bank 1994a).

Targeting women is especially appropriate when doing so contributes directly to reducing poverty or when women have particular needs—for example, when maternal mortality is very high. The exceptionally high gender gap in educational enrollments in some countries can be reduced only by policies (including subsidies) that target girls. An obvious example would be policies that affect the private costs of schooling.

Female household members tend to allocate resources more directly to children, while men tend to allocate more resources to adults.

Reducing these direct costs to households will mean setting new public spending priorities. For example, educational institutions for girls, especially at the primary level, might be exempted from cost recovery measures, thus increasing the implied public spending subsidy to girls. Similarly, a larger number of publicly funded scholarships can be provided for girls, as has been done in Bangladesh and Guatemala.

Opportunity and travel costs can discourage parents from enrolling their children, especially daughters, in school. Some countries have tried to overcome the constraints imposed by opportunity costs by introducing flexible school hours and calendar years and providing child care for younger siblings (box 3.7). In some cases girls who are responsible for looking after their younger brothers and sisters are allowed to bring them to school.

In countries where cultural values may prevent girls from traveling alone to school, measures are needed that will increase access to safe transport,

BOX 3.8 ECONOMIC REFORMS AND GENDER TARGETING IN MONGOLIA

Since Mongolia began its transition to a market economy in 1990, the living conditions of the population have deteriorated dramatically. According to the government's estimates, a quarter of all Mongolians are now living below the poverty line. Single women with young children are among the "new" vulnerable groups that have emerged in the wake of the transition. As of December 1993 nearly 72 percent of households headed by single persons, usually women, were estimated to have incomes below the poverty line. (About 28 percent of all households in Mongolia are headed by women). The Mongolian Women's Federation reports that the divorce rate is rising among jobless low-income couples, increasing the number of single-parent households.

Along with job loss, women are affected by the decline in services such as day care and maternity homes.

Mothers now have to look after their children at home, which restricts their ability to participate in the labor market and, ironically, increases their dependence on welfare. When herds were privatized, priority was given to people who, according to the government, could take better care of the animals. Unfortunately, this policy adversely affected female-headed households.

The maternal mortality rate has doubled over the past three years, in part because many more babies are being delivered at home. Other factors that have contributed to the rising maternal mortality rate include a decrease in the number of ambulances and the need for patients to pay for the food they consume while they are hospitalized.

In Mongolia, targeting female-headed households, pregnant women, and children is essential for reducing poverty. Social assistance, health care, education, and help in finding employment are particularly important (Subbarao and Ezemenari forthcoming).

---

change the geographic distribution of primary schools, or provide more boarding facilities. Projects in Pakistan are using school mapping techniques to establish criteria for placing new schools in currently underserved areas. Such programs benefit both girls and boys.

It may be necessary to target women when economic reforms or systemic transitions are occurring. For example, in Mongolia, as well as in other countries making the transition from a socialist to a market economy, women are disproportionately represented among the unemployed and otherwise disadvantaged (box 3.8). Thus, in designing safety nets to mitigate the short-term negative effects of economic transitions, policymakers need to recognize and evaluate the specific adverse effects on women.

It is not always necessary to restrict a particular program or benefit exclusively to women; the objective can sometimes be achieved indirectly.

Techniques based on self-selection appear to be particularly efficient. In Zambia, where men have a strong preference for cash wages, offering wages in kind (food) attracted more women workers than men to public works programs.

In the financial sector, women entrepreneurs are enabled to borrow at market rates of interest when banking institutions adopt innovative collateral requirements, reduce transaction costs, and offer small loans at repeated intervals. The Grameen Bank in Bangladesh and Badan Kredit Kecamatan in Indonesia do not reserve loans for women specifically; instead, they adopt innovative lending policies the result of which is that women make up the majority of participants—as much as 96 percent in a new branch of the Grameen Bank.

Involving Beneficiaries in Public Policy

Until recently, the absence of input from beneficiaries often left policymakers ignorant about how the costs and benefits of policy changes would be distributed among the population. Today, the views and needs of potential beneficiaries are being taken into account at both the macroeconomic and sectoral levels. This trend should make it possible to determine who benefits, who does not, and why. A good example of a situation in which a beneficiary's point of view can make a significant difference is in public expenditure reviews. Governments with unsustainable budget deficits must make difficult decisions about the allocation of public resources. Their task can often be facilitated by suggestions from the potential beneficiaries themselves, since one of the key questions policymakers face is whether investments as presently allocated are reaching the intended population efficiently and effectively.

Three broad approaches can be used to guarantee that the views of women and other intended beneficiaries are adequately reflected in policy and project formulation. First, surveys and other methods of collecting statistical data can be designed to ensure that gender-disaggregated data are properly collected and analyzed. Second, beneficiary assessments, which use a range of qualitative research methods such as direct observation, selected individual or group interviews, and case studies, can be used to ensure that the views of all groups are adequately represented.

A third approach involves a range of participatory planning and management techniques that reflect a significant transfer of control to the community and local levels. Participatory evaluations use innovative research techniques that allow illiterate and otherwise voiceless groups to express their concerns and priorities. Small grants and credits managed at the local level by NGOs or government agencies permit a community to choose the projects that best reflect its own priorities. Social funds, whereby resources are channeled to demand-driven projects, are one such mechanism. While these participatory approaches have been implemented primarily at the local level, they are also beginning to be used to involve the community in regional and national planning. Participatory methods, by helping to create local capacity, ensure the sustainability of projects and programs. They also help establish rational criteria for making public investment choices that incorporate both social and efficiency objectives.

Generating and Analyzing Gender-Disaggregated Data

Gender-disaggregated data and the capacity to analyze these data provide public policymakers with essential information and enhance the dialogue with agents outside government. One of the most valuable instruments for collecting disaggregated data is the household survey, which can provide detailed information that is invaluable in policymaking. Obtaining full gender-disaggregated information in many instances entails only a small increase in costs, since the disaggregation itself involves little extra work. However, additional resources are often needed to analyze the data and make it useful to policymakers. Public statistical agencies might analyze gender-disaggregated information in partnership with private and academic institutions in order to share the costs.

There are several important steps in collecting useful and accurate gender-disaggregated data. First, in places where gender-disaggregated household data have not yet been collected, special efforts should be made to obtain them. At a minimum, data on how individuals use health and educational services should be collected routinely as part of national consumption and expenditure surveys. If household consumption, income, or production surveys have already been carried out but little or no gender-disaggregated data have been collected, the marginal cost of collection is likely to be quite modest—perhaps on the order of 10 percent of total costs.

Participatory methods help establish rational criteria for making public investment choices that incorporate both social and efficiency objectives.

Second, in places where basic gender-disaggregated data have already been collected, it is important to gather more data from individuals on consumption and, as much as possible, on income and the ownership of assets. Such data are vital for developing a deeper understanding of how access to and allocation and control of resources are determined within households. More data on men's and women's access to credit and information services, such as agricultural extension programs, are needed for an understanding of women's limited access to important production inputs. The data also indicate the effectiveness of projects and programs in providing such services to women.

Third, there should be an increased emphasis on collecting panel data (time series) to facilitate more detailed analyses of changes in household behavior over time. Because full panel surveys are costly, it may be necessary to adopt less-expensive panel methods and combine them with flexible data collection. Anthropological and participatory research methods can be used to enhance the quality and relevance of formal survey questions, as well as to provide a "reality check" on formal survey responses.

Finally, greater priority needs to be given to gender-disaggregated analysis of existing data sets. This analysis should be carried out not only in social sectors such as health and education but also on such issues as the intrahousehold allocation of time and labor and access to and use of productive resources.

Working in Collaboration

Governments' ability to identify and implement policies that promote gender equality is greatly enhanced by the active participation of other players from the development community and civil society. These agents include individual women and men, community-based groups, private for-profit firms, trade unions, nongovernmental organizations, and multilateral and bilateral agencies. Interaction between public institutions and other actors provides the basis for a more informed policy dialogue on gender issues. It also lays the foundation for operational collaboration and for broadly based support for public policy measures.

Over the past several decades NGOs have become major players in international development. NGOs are by no means homogenous. In the field of development, they range from large volunteer and charity organizations, many of them based in industrial countries, to community-based self-help groups. They also include research institutes, volunteer-sending agencies, religious organizations, professional associations, and lobbying groups.

NGOs concerned with gender issues have had a particularly important role in designing and implementing gender programs, especially at the grassroots level, and in advocating policy change at the national level. NGOs have been effective in providing information and education to women and in helping community-based women's organizations lobby for change. In many countries collaboration between NGOs and governments is still relatively new. Nonetheless, it is growing rapidly—most visibly in the delivery of social and financial services.

For example, in Peru a proposed basic health and nutrition project aims to improve the quality and accessibility of health and nutritional services, with an emphasis on poor women and children. NGOs are expected to play a major role in implementing the project and will be responsible for 75 percent of training and research, 40 percent of education, and 20 percent of service delivery (World Bank 1994g). In Africa many HIV/AIDS support programs are managed by NGOs, with assistance from governments and funds from international donors.

In the long run the choices made by private sector agents are profoundly important for the persistence or reduction of gender inequalities.

In the financial services sector NGOs have found innovative ways of overcoming barriers that women face in access to credit and savings facilities. Among the better-known programs are the Grameen Bank in Bangladesh, ACCION International in Latin America, and the NGO consortium ACCORD in Africa. NGOs have been very successful in organizing village banks and mobile banking systems to reach the rural poor. These credit programs provide women not only with the funds to finance income-generating activities but also with opportunities to acquire basic business skills and to assume leadership positions within their peer groups.

Governments also seek to collaborate with a range of institutions from the private sector. In the long run the choices made by private sector agents—whether households, firms, or trade unions—are profoundly important for the persistence or reduction of gender inequalities. Joint public–private sector initiatives can be vital in changing people's perceptions about the benefits of investing in or hiring women. The private sector has a comparative advantage in providing certain kinds of services to women—for example, vocational education and training. Collaboration with the private sector often means that public resources can be reallocated to those investments that offer the highest rate of social return, such as basic education and health care.

Strengthening International Policies to Meet New Challenges

Not all issues that bear on gender equality can be effectively addressed by individual nations. For example, refugee and displaced women and children account for up to 80 percent of the 50 million refugees and displaced persons worldwide. The sheer numbers of refugee and displaced women and children highlight the urgent need to devise international strategies for dealing with this problem.

The sheer numbers of refugee and displaced women and children (estimated at 40 million) highlight the urgent need to devise international strategies for dealing with this problem.

The constraints that refugee and displaced women face are similar to those faced by other women, only magnified many times. They lack access to health services, even though their health risks are high. Girls often have less access to basic education than in their home countries. With little access to family planning, women's fertility rates may be extraordinarily high at a time when the burden of additional children hinders the chances of survival for both mothers and infants. In the absence of professional abortion services, women may rely on self-induced and unsafe abortions. The proportion of female-headed households is highest in refugee situations, yet the women's income-generating activities and skills are minimal.

The international response to this type of crisis is usually limited to emergency relief measures. Although vital, these measures often fail to recognize the long-term economic and social costs involved in restructuring the lives of displaced women when they return to their home countries. International public policy has an important role in preparing refugee and displaced women for their future role in rebuilding their societies. Long-term repatriation and development on a regional basis along the lines of the International Conference on Central American Refugees (CIREFCA) in Central America is one approach to involving governments, NGOs, and development agencies in a coordinated response to refugee problems.[8] Governments and agencies must make every effort to collaborate in making repatriation viable by establishing development programs that explicitly take account of refugees' needs. Otherwise, chances are high that people will once again be forced to leave their countries, putting at risk national reconciliation efforts.

Another area that demands an international response is the establishment of legal conventions for the enforcement of social justice and human rights. Equality under the law creates the legitimacy policymakers and private individuals need to seek change that will increase well-being and encourage economic opportunity. In certain instances, legitimacy needs to be established at the international level. For this reason, it is vitally important that governments ratify the Convention on the Elimination of All Forms of Discrimination against Women. This convention, adopted by the United Nations General Assembly in 1979, provides a framework for action by countries to reduce discrimination against women in political and public life, law and education, employment, health care, commerce, and domestic relations. International conventions of this type provide an important policy lever for women's organizations and other groups in civil society.

Conclusions

This chapter has presented the rationale for public interventions to promote gender equality. Such interventions are needed because of market failures and social externalities that extend beyond the individual household to affect society in general. For resources to be allocated efficiently, public spending should focus on those investments with the highest social returns. Given the evidence of high social and private returns to investments in women's human capital, public expenditures should give priority to the investments that have the largest impact on the welfare of girls and women, especially in basic education and reproductive and other health care services. Policymakers also need to identify areas in which actions can be taken that would have gender-neutral outcomes, including sectoral programs addressing transport and infrastructure, water supply, and sanitation.

By directing public resources toward policies and projects that reduce gender inequality, policymakers are promoting not only equality today but also higher labor productivity, a higher rate of human capital formation, slower population growth, and stronger economic growth tomorrow.

Governments can no longer afford not to invest in women. The evidence on private and social returns to investments in women and girls cannot be ignored. By directing public resources toward policies and projects that reduce gender inequality, policymakers are promoting not only equality today but also higher labor productivity, a higher rate of human capital formation, slower population growth, and stronger economic growth tomorrow. However, none of these goals can be reached without the participation of women themselves. Governments and collaborating institutions must listen carefully to the voices of individual women, to women's groups, and to woman policymakers. By working with others to identify and implement policies for greater gender equality, governments can take actions that will make a real difference to the future well-being and prosperity of their people.

Notes

1. Birdsall and Sabot (1994) use earlier findings by Barro (1991) to test the relationship between inequality and growth. They find that in Latin America unequal distribution of education, in terms of both quality and quantity, constrained economic growth in the region by reducing opportunities for increasing labor productivity. In East Asia open and relatively equal access to high-quality basic education led to a virtuous circle of high educational performance that stimulated growth and reduced inequality.

2. Subbarao and Raney (1993) estimate that a doubling of family planning services in 1982 would have reduced the fertility rate from 5.5 to 5.0 and the number of births by 3.5 percent.

3. The Living Standards Measurement Study (LSMS) is a series of multitopic surveys designed to study multiple aspects of household welfare.

4. Deforestation is represented by the time required to collect a standard load of fuelwood.

5. It would be more illuminating to compare wage differences across three categories of women workers: women without children; women with children but with no interruption in employment except for statutory maternity leave; and women with children and with interrupted employment.

6. Among women workers, 53 percent are in commerce, compared with 33 percent of men. In manufacturing, 16 percent of the workers are men, compared with 14 percent for women. In services, 37 percent are men and 33 percent are women (World Bank 1995c).

7. In Bolivia informal moneylenders require borrowers to write postdated checks. If borrowers fail to make timely repayments, these checks are deposited and, as the lender knows, will bounce for lack of funds. A bounced check is a criminal offense in Bolivia, and the lender can have the borrower arrested. The World Bank estimates that about 20 percent of all Bolivian prison inmates—and 40 percent of female inmates—are imprisoned for "bouncing" checks and for other collateral-related crimes. In many cases children must live in prison with their mothers (Winkler and Guedes 1995).

8. The International Conference on Central American Refugees (CIREFCA) was held in Guatemala City in May 1989. A total of 126 projects in seven countries were introduced, with an overall investment of $365 million. Areas with high densities of returnees were targeted, and special attention was given to projects to support displaced women.

References

Agarwal, Bina. 1994. "Gender and Command Over Property: A Critical Gap in Economic Analysis and Policy in South Asia." *World Development* 22(10):1455–78.

Baden, Sally. 1993. "The Impact of Recession and Structural Adjustment on Women's Work in Developing and Developed Countries." Working paper. International Labour Office, Geneva.

Bardhan, Kalpana. 1993. "Women and Rural Poverty: Some Asian Cases." In M. G. Quibria, ed., *Rural Poverty in Asia: Priority Issues and Policy Options.* New York: Oxford University Press.

Bardhan, Pranab. 1988. "Sex Disparity in Child Survival in Rural India." In T. Srinivasan and Pranab Bardhan, eds., *Rural Poverty in South Asia.* New York: Columbia University Press.

Barro, Robert. 1991. "Economic Growth in a Cross-section of Countries." *Quarterly Journal of Economics* 106 (May):407–43.

Beneria, Lourdes. 1992. "Accounting for Women's Work: The Progress of Two Decades." *World Development* 20(11):1547–60.

Bindlish, Vishva, and Robert Evenson. 1993. *Evaluation of the Performance of T and V Extension in Kenya.* World Bank Technical Paper 208. Washington, D.C.

Binswanger, Hans, and Mark R. Rosenzweig, eds. 1984. *Contractual Arrangements, Employment and Wages in Rural Labor Markets in Asia.* New Haven, Conn.: Yale University Press.

Birdsall, Nancy, and Richard Sabot. 1994. "Inequality as a Constraint on Growth." Working Paper. Manila: Asian Development Bank.

Blau, Francine, and Lawrence N. Kahn. 1992. "The Gender Earnings Gap: Learning from International Comparisons." *American Economic Review* 82(2):533–38.

Bouis, Howarth E., and Eileen T. Kennedy. 1989. "Traditional Cash Crop Schemes' Effects on Production, Consumption and Nutrition: Sugarcane in the Philippines and Kenya." Prepared for IFPRI-INCAP Policy Workshop, Antigua, Guatemala.

Chatterjee, Meera. 1991. *Indian Women: Their Health and Productivity.* World Bank Discussion Paper 109. Washington, D.C.

David, Rosalind. 1992. *The Effects of Male Out-migration on Women's Management of the Natural Resource Base of the Sahel.* SOS International, London.

Donors to African Education. 1994. *A Statistical Profile of Education in Sub-Saharan Africa in the 1980s.* Paris.

Duraiswamy, P. 1992. "Child Survival, Preventive Health Care and Schooling in Rural Households of Tamil Nadu: India." Yale University, New Haven, Conn.

Edgerton, V. R., G. W. Gardner, Y. Ohira, K. A. Gunarwardena, and B. Senewiratne. 1979. "Iron Deficiency Anaemia and Its Effects on Worker Productivity and Activity Patterns." *British Medical Journal* 2:1546–49.

Einhorn, Barbara. 1993. *Cinderella Goes to Market: Citizenship, Gender and Women's Movements in East Central Europe.* London: Verso.

FAO (Food and Agriculture Organization). 1993. *Rural Poverty Alleviation: Policies and Trends.* Economic and Social Development Paper 113. Rome.

Fields, Gary S. 1992. "Changing Poverty and Inequality in Latin America." *Public Finance* 47 (Supplement):59–76.

Folbre, Nancy. 1994. *Who Pays for the Kids? Gender and the Structures of Constraint.* London: Routledge.

Fong, Monica. 1993. *The Role of Women in Rebuilding the Russian Economy.* Studies of Economics in Transformation 10. Washington, D.C.: World Bank.

Goetz, Anne Marie, and Rina Sen Gupta. 1994. "Who Takes the Credit? Gender, Power and Control over Loan Use in Rural Credit Programmes in Bangladesh." Draft. University of Sussex, Institute of Development Studies, Brighton, U.K.

Hart, Gillian. 1986. *Power, Labor, and Livelihood: Processes of Change in Rural Java.* San Francisco: University of Berkeley Press.

Heise, Lori. 1993. "Violence Against Women: The Missing Agenda." In Marge Koblinsky, Judith Timyan, and Jill Gay, eds., *The Health of Women: A Global Perspective.* Boulder, Colo.: Westview.

Heise, Lori, Jacqueline Pitanguy, and Adrienne Germain. 1994. *Violence Against Women: The Hidden Health Burden.* World Bank Discussion Paper 255. Washington, D.C.

Herz, Barbara, and Shahidur Khandker. 1991. *Women's Work, Education, and Family Welfare in Peru.* World Bank Discussion Paper 116. Washington, D.C.

Herz, Barbara, K. Subbarao, Masooma Habib, and Laura Raney. 1991. *Letting Girls Learn: Promising Approaches in Primary and Secondary Education.* World Bank Discussion Paper 133. Washington, D.C.

Hoddinot, John, and Lawrence Haddad. 1992. "Does Female Income-share Influence Household Expenditures? Evidence from Côte d'Ivoire." Trinity College, Oxford University, Oxford, U.K.

Holt, Sharon. 1995. "Gender and Property Rights: Women and Agrarian Reform in Russia and Moldova." World Bank, Europe and Central Asia Region, Washington, D.C.

Holt, Sharon, and Helena Ribe. 1991. *Developing Financial Institutions for the Poor and Reducing Barriers to Access for Women.* World Bank Discussion Paper 117. Washington, D.C.

Horton, Susan. 1994. "Women and Industrialization in Asia." University of Toronto, Institute for Policy Analysis.

Hosken, Fran P., ed. 1992. *Women's International Network (WIN) News.* 18(4).

ILO/INSTRAW. 1985. *Women in Economic Activity: A Global Statistical Survey 1950–2000.* Geneva.

Jackson, Cecile. 1993. "Doing What Comes Naturally? Women and Environment in Development." *World Development* 21(12):1947–63.

Johansen, Frida. 1993. *Poverty Reduction in East Asia.* World Bank Discussion Paper 203. Washington, D.C.

Jurisman, Clara, and Araceli Moreno. 1990. "Women, Labour and Crisis: Mexico." Prepared for International Center for Research on Women (ICRW) project on Weathering Economic Crises: Women's Economic Responses to Recession in Latin America and the Caribbean. ICRW, Washington, D.C.

Kalima, Rose. 1992. *Where Women are Leaders: The SEWA Movement in India.* London: Zed Press.

Khandker, Shahidur R., and Osman H. Chowdhury. 1994. "Targeted Credit Programs and Rural Poverty in Bangladesh." World Bank, Education and Social Policy Department, Washington, D.C., and Bangladesh Institute of Development Studies, Dhaka.

Khandker, Shahidur R., and Baqui Khalily. 1995. "Designing a Sustainable Poverty Alleviation Program: The BRAC Strategy in Bangladesh." World Bank, Education and Social Policy Department, Washington, D.C., and Bangladesh Institute of Development Studies, Dhaka.

Khandker, Shahidur R., Baqui Khalily, and Zahed Khan. 1993. "Sustainability of Grameen Bank: What Do We Know?" World Bank, Education and Social Policy Department, Washington, D.C., and Bangladesh Institute of Development Studies, Dhaka.

Khandker, Shahidur R., Victor Lavy, and D. Filmer. 1994. *Schooling and Cognitive Achievements of Children in Morocco.* World Bank Discussion Paper 264. Washington, D.C.

Kumar, Shubh K., and David Hotchkiss. 1988. *Consequences of Deforestation for Women's Time Allocation, Agricultural Production, and Nutrition in Hill Areas of Nepal.* International Food Policy Research Institute Research Report 69. Washington, D.C.

Kuznets, Simon. 1955. "Economic Growth and Income Inequalities." *American Economic Review* 45 (March):1–28.

Lavy, Victor. 1992. *Investment in Human Capital: Schooling Supply Constraints in Rural Ghana.* Living Standards Measurement Study Working Paper 93. Washington, D.C.: World Bank.

MacDonald, Martha. 1994. "Panel Presentation at the Gender Symposium." World Bank, Poverty and Social Policy Department, Washington, D.C.

Manser, Marilyn, and Murray Brown. 1980. "Marriage and Household Decision-making: A Bargaining Analysis." *International Economic Review* 21:31–44.

McElroy, Marjorie, and Mary Jean Horney. 1981. "Nash-bargained Household Decisions: Towards a Generalisation of the Theory of Demand." *International Economic Review* 22 (June):333–49.

Moock, Peter R. 1976. "The Efficiency of Women as Farm Managers: Kenya." *American Journal of Agricultural Economics* 58(5):831–35.

Moser, Caroline O. 1992. "Adjustment from Below: Low-income Women, Time and the Triple Role in Guayaquil, Ecuador." In Haleh Afshar and Carolynne Dennis, eds., *Women and Adjustment Policies in the Third World.* New York: St. Martin's Press.

_____. 1994. "Urban Poverty and Social Policy in the Context of Adjustment." World Bank, Urban Development Division, Washington, D.C.

Mwabu, Germano. 1994. "Household Composition and Expenditures on Human Capital Inputs in Kenya." Presented at Northeast Universities Development Conference, Economic Growth Center. Yale University, New Haven, Conn.

Newell, Andrew, and Barry Reilly. 1994. "The Gender Wage Gap in Russia." World Bank, Europe and Central Asia Country Department 3, Washington, D.C.

Pitt, Mark, and Shahidur Khandker. 1995. "Household and Intrahousehold Impacts of the Grameen Bank and Similar Targeted Credited Programs in Bangladesh." World Bank, Education and Social Policy Department, Washington, D.C.

Population Reference Bureau. 1994. *The World's Youth 1994: A Special Focus on Reproductive Health.* Washington, D.C.

Psacharopoulos, George. 1994. "Returns to Investment in Education: A Global Update." *World Development* 22(9):1325–43.

Psacharopoulos, George, and Zafiris Tzannatos. 1992. *Women's Employment and Pay in Latin America: Overview and Methodology.* A World Bank Regional and Sectoral Study. Washington, D.C.

Quisumbing, Agnes. 1994. "Improving Women's Agricultural Productivity as Farmers and Workers." Education and Social Policy Department Discussion Paper 37. World Bank, Washington, D.C.

Rahman, Rushidan I., and Shahidur Khandker. 1994. "Role of Targeted Credit Programs in Promoting Employment and Productivity of the Poor in Bangladesh." World Bank, Education and Social Policy Department, Washington, D.C., and Bangladesh Institute of Development Studies, Dhaka.

Rhyne, Elisabeth, and Sharon Holt. 1994. "Women in Finance and Enterprise Development." Education and Social Policy Department Discussion Paper 40. World Bank, Washington, D.C.

Rosenzweig, Mark, and T. Paul Schultz. 1982. "Market Opportunities, Genetic Endowments, and Intrafamily Resource Distribution: Child Survival in Rural India." *American Economic Review* 72:4:803–15.

_____. 1987. "Fertility and Investments in Human Capital: Estimates of the Consequences of Imperfect Fertility Control in Malaysia." *Journal of Econometrics* 36:163–84.

Saito, Katrine, and Daphne Spurling. 1992. *Developing Agricultural Extension for Women Farmers.* World Bank Discussion Paper 156. Washington, D.C.

Scales, Ann. 1986. "The Emergence of Feminist Jurisprudence." *Yale Law Journal* 95(7):1373–1403.

Schuler, Margaret, ed. 1986. *Empowerment and the Law: Strategies of Third World Women.* Washington, D.C.: OEF International.

Schuler, Margaret, and Sakuntala Kadirgamar-Rajasingham, eds. 1992. *Legal Literacy: A Tool for Women's Empowerment.* New York: United Nations Development Fund for Women (UNIFEM).

Schultz, T. Paul. 1988. "Education Investments and Returns." In Hollis Chenery and T. R. Srinivasan, eds., *Handbook of Development Economics*. Amsterdam: North-Holland.

Sedlacek, Guilherme, Leah Gutierrez, and Amit Mohindra. 1993. "Women in the Labor Market." World Bank, Education and Social Policy Department, Washington, D.C.

Sen, Amartya. 1990. "More Than One Hundred Million Women Are Missing: Women's Survival as a Development Problem." *New York Review of Books* (December 20):61–66.

Sivard, R. L. 1985. *Women: A World Survey.* Washington, D.C.: World Priorities.

Stewart, Sheelagh. 1992. "Working the System: Sensitizing the Police to the Plight of Women." In Margaret Schuler, ed., *Freedom from Violence: Women's Strategies from around the World.* New York: United Nations Development Fund for Women (UNIFEM).

Subbarao Kalanidhi, and Kene Ezemenari. Forthcoming. "Transition, Poverty and Social Assistance in Mongolia." World Bank, Education and Social Policy Department. Washington, D.C.

Subbarao Kalanidhi, and Laura Raney. 1993. *Social Gains from Female Education: A Cross-National Study.* World Bank Discussion Paper 194. Washington, D.C.

Summers, Lawrence H. 1994. *Investing in All the People: Educating Women in Developing Countries.* EDI Seminar Paper 45. Washington, D.C.: World Bank.

Thomas, Duncan. 1990a. "Household Resources and Child Health in Zimbabwe." Working Paper. Yale University, Economic Growth Center, New Haven, Conn.

_____. 1990b. "Intrahousehold Resource Allocation: An Inferential Approach." *Journal of Human Resources* 25(4):635–64.

_____. 1991. *Gender Differences in Household Resource Allocation.* Living Standards Measurement Study Working Paper 79. Washington, D.C.: World Bank.

_____. 1993. "The Distribution of Income and Expenditure within the Household." *Annals of Economics and Statistics* 29:109–35.

Tibaijuka, Anna. 1994. "Cost of Differential Gender Roles in African Agriculture: A Case Study of Smallholder Banana-Coffee Farms in the Kagera Region, Tanzania." *Journal of Agricultural Economics* (U.K.) 45(1):69–81.

Toubia, Nahid. 1993. *Female Genital Mutilation: A Call for Global Action.* New York: United Nations.

Tzannatos, Zafiris. 1995. "Growth, Adjustment, and the Labor Market: Effects on Women Workers." World Bank, Poverty and Social Policy Department, Washington, D.C.

UNESCO (United Nations Educational, Scientific, and Cultural Organization). 1991. *Statistical Yearbook 1991.* Paris.

_____. 1993a. *Statistical Yearbook 1993.* Paris.

_____. 1993b. *Trends and Projections of Enrollment by Level of Education by Age and Sex, 1960–2025.* Paris.

UNICEF (United Nations Children's Fund). 1993. *The Progress of Nations.* New York.

UNIDO (United Nations Industrial Development Organization). 1993. *Women in Manu-*

facturing: Participation Patterns, Determinants and Trends. Unit for the Integration of Women in Industrial Development. Vienna.

United Nations. 1991. *The World's Women 1970–1990: Trends and Statistics.* New York.

_____. 1993. *World Population Prospects: The 1992 Revision.* New York.

Van de Walle, Dominique, and Kimberley Nead, eds. 1995. "Public Spending and the Poor: Theory and Evidence." World Bank, Policy Research Department, Washington, D.C. (To be published for the World Bank by the Johns Hopkins University Press, Baltimore, Md.)

WHO (World Health Organization). 1994. *Women and AIDS: Agenda for Action.* Geneva.

Wickramasinghe, A. 1992. "Women's Role in Rural Households and Agriculture in Sri Lanka." In J. H. Momsen, ed., *Geographical Studies in Women and Development.* London: Routledge.

Winkler, Donald, and Andrea Guedes. 1995. "Enhancing Women's Contribution to Economic Development in Latin America and the Caribbean: The World Bank's Experience." World Bank, Technical Department, Latin America and the Caribbean Region, Washington, D.C.

Winter, Carolyn. 1994. "Gender Discrimination in the Labor Market and the Role of the Law: Experiences in Six Latin American Countries." World Bank, Latin America and the Caribbean Region, Technical Department, Washington, D.C.

World Bank. 1993. *World Development Report 1993: Investing in Health.* New York: Oxford University Press.

_____. 1994a. *Enhancing Women's Participation in Economic Development.* A World Bank Policy Paper. Washington, D.C.

_____. 1994b. *A New Agenda for Women's Health and Nutrition.* Washington, D.C.

_____. 1994c. *Enriching Lives: Overcoming Vitamin and Mineral Malnutrition in Developing Countries.* World Bank.

_____. 1994d. "Regulatory Costs and Employment in the Informal Sector of Argentina." Education and Social Policy Department Discussion Paper 45. World Bank, Washington, D.C.

_____. 1994e. "Rural Women in the Sahel and Their Access to Agricultural Extension: Overview of Five Country Case Studies." Agricultural Operations Division, Sahelian Department, Washington, D.C.

_____. 1994f. *World Development Report 1994: Infrastructure for Development.* New York: Oxford University Press.

_____. 1994g. "World Bank Sourcebook on Participation." Social Policy and Resettlement Division, Washington, D.C.

_____. 1995a. "Cameroon: Diversity, Growth and Poverty Reduction." Africa Technical Department, Washington, D.C.

_____. 1995b. *Investing in People.* Washington, D.C.

_____. 1995c. "Poverty, Deregulation, and Employment in the Informal Sector of Mexico." Education and Social Policy Department, Washington, D.C.

Yaron, Jacob. 1992. *Successful Rural Finance Institutions.* World Bank Discussion Paper 150. Washington, D.C.

Other Recent Development in Practice Books